A Dash & a Dollop

Every recipe tells a story.

Recipes are some of the most cherished parts of our family legacies. **A Dash & a Dollop** is our way of celebrating the unique life stories of our residents and their families.

We hope you enjoy reading and using this recipe book as much as we enjoyed creating it.

Sharing Memories from the Kitchen

In the Atria kitchen, one of our favorite things to do is try recipes our residents share with us. We've even added some of these dishes to our regular menus for everyone to enjoy. After years of preparing these recipes, we've discovered that Atria is home to many great cooks who could teach us all a thing or two.

We've also realized just how deeply meaningful these recipes are to our residents and their families. Many of their most vivid memories involve food – cooking in the kitchen with family and friends, sharing wonderful meals and lively conversation around the table, or passing down recipes for future generations.

To celebrate the important role these culinary experiences play in the lives of those who call Atria home, we are honored to present *A Dash & a Dollop* – a special collection of cherished family recipes and the stories behind them.

We asked you – Atria residents and family members – and Atria staff to share your favorite recipes and tell us what they mean for your family. The response was remarkable. Hundreds of recipes and stories were submitted from across the country – we've included as many of them as we could here for you and future generations to enjoy.

A Dash & a Dollop is truly a labor of love. Thank you for allowing Atria to be a part of your family story.

Ronda Watson, RD

Ronda Watson, RD
Vice President of Culinary Services
Atria Senior Living

Table of Contents

The recipes included in this book have not been tested for accuracy and are based on the recollection and memories of residents and their family members.

Appetizers

Tantalizing soups that simmer on the stove for hours until they're just right. Zesty dips that get the conversation going before dinner. Savory bites that make a couple's first cocktail party a success.

Artichoke Dip

Prep Time: 10 minutes | Cook Time: 20 – 25 minutes | Servings: 10

ngredients:

2 (14 oz.) cans of artichokes, in water

2 c. parmesan cheese, freshly grated

1 c. mayonnaise

garlic powder to taste

Preparation:

Drain artichokes and coarsely chop.

Combine artichokes, cheese, mayonnaise and garlic in an oven-safe serving dish.

Bake at 350°F until bubbly and light brown on top.

Serve with toasted, thinly sliced French baguette, raw vegetables or chips.

My daughter, Joan, moved to Atlanta in 1976, where she shopped in a specialty grocery store. The store was an elegant place; the floors were carpeted and chandeliers hung from the ceiling. At that time, this market had scanners to check out groceries; very advanced for 1976! Joan picked up this recipe at that market. It is a family favorite at holiday parties!

Muriel Siskind, Atria Stamford resident

Black Radish Delight

Prep Time: 60 minutes | Servings: 3 – 5

Ingredients:

- 3 large black radishes
- 1 tbsp. salt (for preparation only)
- 2 sweet onions
- 2 long bunches of scallions
- ½ c. olive oil
- salt and pepper to taste

Preparation:

Peel radishes until they are snowy white and grate them on the large size of a grater.

Put the grated radishes in a large bowl of water with a spoonful of salt, for about an hour. After they are soaked, place in a colander and rinse with cold water. Squeeze them thoroughly until dry.

Peel and dice the onions. Clean and dice the scallions, including the heads.

Combine onions and scallions with radishes. Mix olive oil until mixture is moistened.

Add salt and pepper to taste. Chill in refrigerator. Serve with main course or with bread.

If there was one dish the Klapper Clan loved, it was the black radish delight. The original recipe was handed down by my grandparents, who came from Poland. The story told by my grandmother was that in those days, back in Poland, winters were harsh and they had to do the best they could with what they found. Radishes were easy to find and were inexpensive. It was the first dish to be served at all family dinners and holidays; a Klapper trademark dish.

Marvin Klapper, Atria Lynbrook resident

Broad Bean Cream Soup

Cook Time: 25 minutes | Servings: 8

ngredients:

2 c. shelled yellow broad beans, uncooked

4 – 6 c. water

½ c. butter

1 garlic clove

2 tbsp. chicken or tomato bouillon

salt and pepper to taste

Preparation:

Boil broad beans in water until cooked through. If using dried beans, cook according to package directions.

Purée the cooked broad beans and water in a blender until they are thick and creamy.

Place in a large cooking pot on high heat.

Add butter, garlic and bouillon. Stir until butter is melted and bouillon is evenly distributed.

Add salt and pepper to taste. Boil for 10 minutes and add water according to desired thickness.

As a teenager, I had to have all four of my molars extracted and was limited to a liquid diet for a week. My mom had to think creatively and provide something nutritional, yet filling. So one afternoon, she whipped up a big pot of this delicious soup! She just decided to add a dash of this and a dollop of that. Years later, living on my own in a different country, I once came upon bags of shelled yellow broad beans at a local Mexican supermarket. I tried a dash of this, a dollop of that and got a taste of home.

Andrea De Lara, Atria Burlingame Engage Life Director

Buffalo Chicken Dip

Prep Time: 10 minutes | Cook Time: 30 minutes | Servings: 10 – 15

Ingredients:

- 2 skinless, boneless chicken breasts, cooked and chopped (or use about 2 cups of chicken pulled from a rotisserie chicken)
- 16 oz. Frank's® hot sauce
- 12 oz. cream cheese
- 1 c. ranch dressing
- 2 c. sharp cheddar cheese, grated

Preparation:

Soak the chicken in the Frank's hot sauce for 1 – 2 hours.

Drain off some of the excess hot sauce and mix in all other ingredients.

Bake in the oven at 350°F for 30 minutes. Serve with celery and Fritos.®

We have to serve this at every Jessee family gathering or the family gets very upset. At Thanksgiving, two batches are needed!

Mark and Diane Jessee,
Atria Senior Living Chief Financial Officer and his wife

Cheese Puffs

Prep Time: 15 minutes | Cook Time: 15 – 20 minutes | Servings: 4

Ingredients:

2 c. American cheese, shredded

1 stick of butter

2 c. flour

¼ tsp. paprika

¼ tsp. salt

Preparation:

Mix cheese and butter together at room temperature.

Blend in flour, paprika and salt.

Shape into balls. (Balls may be frozen on a cookie sheet and stored in a plastic bag.)

Bake 2" apart on a cookie sheet at 350°F for 15 – 20 minutes. Serve hot.

The first time I visited my husband's cousin and his wife Barbara, I discovered that she was a marvelous hostess and cook. We were served her cheese puffs appetizer before a delicious dinner. Later, when Barbara moved to Arizona, she and I remained good friends. She continued to cook wonderful meals even after being stricken with rheumatoid arthritis, when it was painful to work the dough with her hands. Even when standing and walking became difficult for her, she managed to raise three children, work full-time and cook almost every day. She's since passed away, but every time I have these cheese puffs I think of Barbara and what a strong person she was.

Story submitted by Paula Blum, pictured here with her mother, Atria Lynbrook resident Marlene Weiss

Chicken Soup

Prep Time: 15 minutes | Cook Time: 45 minutes | Servings: 8

Ingredients:

4 lb. chicken, whole
8 c. water
1 lb. raw carrots, sliced
4 large yellow onions, chopped
6 stalks celery, chopped
1 cube chicken bouillon
salt and pepper to taste
3 – 4 sprigs fresh dill
½ bunch of parsley

Preparation:

Wash chicken and remove excess fat. Put chicken into 6-quart pot. Add 6 cups water; let that come to a boil. Remove the froth. Let simmer on low heat for 45 minutes, or until chicken is cooked through and falling apart.

Remove chicken from pot. Remove the skin and discard. Pull chicken apart and set the meat aside.

Strain broth and add back into the pot. Add 2 more cups of water. Add carrots, onions, celery and bouillon, then salt and pepper to taste. Let that come to a boil. Reduce heat and add dill and parsley. Cook until carrots and onions are done. Remove from heat and serve.

Every time we were sick, we would call Mom to make this special chicken soup. It was Jewish Penicillin. If she didn't have a chicken, she would go out and buy one. This soup heals every time.

Jackie DeSpautz, Atria Palm Desert resident

Chow-Chow Relish

Prep Time: 45 minutes | Cook Time: 45 minutes | Servings: 6 pints

Ingredients:

8 – 10 green tomatoes
4 – 6 heads of cabbage
6 – 8 bell peppers

Preparation:

Finely chop all ingredients. Place together in a large, deep pot and add enough water to cover.

Stir frequently; be sure not to scorch the bottom. Cook approximately 45 minutes until tender.

Relish is used as a topping on mustard greens, vegetables, bread or anything you wish.

As a young bride, I knew nothing about cooking but my husband, Joe, had three older sisters who were accomplished cooks. I received a recipe from the eldest sister-in-law for chow-chow relish. My husband always had a beautiful garden full of these ingredients and he helped prepare the relish – but he drew the line at 12 dozen of each ingredient!

Agnes Greak, Atria Collier Park resident

Crab Dip

Prep Time: 10 minutes | Cook Time: 25 minutes | Servings: 8

Ingredients:

8 oz. cream cheese
6 oz. can crab meat
1 tbsp. milk
¼ tbsp. horseradish
¼ tbsp. salt
dash of pepper
1 c. almonds, slivered
1 loaf French bread, round

Preparation:

Combine the cream cheese, crab meat, milk, horseradish, salt, pepper and almonds.

Spread mixture in baking dish and bake for 15 minutes at 375°F.

While dip is baking, remove the top of the loaf of round French bread and hollow out some of the soft bread.

Remove baked crab dip from the oven and stir well.

Spoon the mixture into the bread bowl you've made, bake an additional 10 minutes and enjoy!

I would serve this dip at all of my parties. The gals would get together and each bring something. I would always make this dip, which everyone loved. It reminds me of all the fun times my girlfriends and I shared together and I hope you will enjoy it as much as we did.

Ava Jensen, Atria Hillcrest resident

Deviled Eggs

Prep Time: 45 minutes | Cook Time: 25 minutes | Servings: 12

Ingredients:

- 1 dozen eggs
- 2 tsp. onion
- 2 tsp. pimento
- 1 tsp. salt
- ¼ tsp. pepper
- 1 tsp. celery seed
- 1 tsp. vinegar
- 1 tbsp. mustard
- 2 tbsp. pickle relish
- 3 tbsp. mayonnaise
- dash of Tabasco® sauce

Preparation:

To boil eggs, place in tepid water and bring to boil for a total of 25 minutes, starting from the time the eggs are placed in the water.

Cool immediately under cold running water and let eggs sit for 30 minutes. Peel off the eggshells.

Cut eggs in half longways and remove egg yolks to a separate bowl. Mix all other ingredients with egg yolks.

Stuff egg whites with egg yolk mixture.

Back in 1950, my mother was newly married and new to the kitchen. She was the third girl in a family of five children. Her mother and two older sisters did all the cooking. Mother's family was going on a picnic and she didn't know what to bring as her contribution to the meal. Her mother told her there was a recipe in the *Courier-Journal* newspaper for deviled eggs and she should try making them. Mom went on to have seven children and made many meals in her lifetime. Whenever there was a potluck occasion in the family, mother was always there with her deviled eggs.

Anne Greene, pictured here with her mother,
Atria Stony Brook resident Martha Steinbock Pike

Honeydew Lime Soup

Prep Time: 20 minutes | Servings: 4 – 6

Ingredients:

½ honeydew melon

¾ c. water

¼ c. frozen limeade concentrate

4 oz. vanilla yogurt

Preparation:

Peel and remove insides from ½ a honeydew melon and blend in food processor until smooth.

Add water and frozen limeade concentrate, then blend again. Stir in vanilla yogurt.

Cover and chill at least 1 hour before serving. Serve cold.

Everyone loves hot soup, but in my family we liked cold soup for summertime. In Los Angeles, the summers were hot, so I experimented with making cold soups from the fruit we had growing in our backyard. Here is a good one we came up with!

Bee Mandell, Atria El Camino Gardens resident

Kale Soup

Prep Time: 30 minutes | Cook Time: 2 hours | Servings: 6 – 8

ngredients:

1 lb. linguiça sausage, sliced ½" thick
1 lb. beef shank, cross-cut
1 onion, chopped
4 beef bouillon cubes
3 – 5 potatoes, peeled and cubed
4 – 5 carrots, peeled and sliced into 1" pieces
1 can red kidney beans, drained
1 bunch kale, trimmed and torn into 1" pieces

Preparation:

In a large soup pot, add sausage, whole beef shank, onion, bouillon cubes and water to fill at least ½ full.

Simmer 1 hour. Remove beef from bone and chop meat, then return meat to pot.

Add potatoes, carrots and beans. Simmer about 30 minutes.

Test for doneness and adjust seasonings.

Add kale, cover and simmer 15 more minutes.

Enjoy with Portuguese bread.

This recipe came to our family from a Portuguese grandma who lived in New Bedford, Massachusetts and was a friend of the family. We haven't changed the recipe at all and have enjoyed it for decades! My grandchildren now make the same recipe the same way.

Jeanne C. Yehle, Atria Draper Place resident

Marinated Seafood with Red Onion

Prep Time: 30 minutes | Servings: 15 – 20

Ingredients:

- 1 ¼ lbs. shrimp, lobster or crab, cooked
- 2 red onions, sliced in thin rings, separated
- 8 oz. tomato sauce
- 1 c. red vinegar
- ¼ c. vegetable oil
- 2 tbsp. sugar
- garlic to taste, crushed
- 1 tsp. Worcestershire sauce
- 1 tsp. salt
- ½ tsp. paprika
- ½ tsp. pepper
- juice of 2 lemons

Preparation:

If you choose to use shrimp, use medium-sized whole shrimp. If you choose lobster or crab, break into bite-sized morsels.

Combine all ingredients and place in a covered dish. Allow to marinate in refrigerator at least 3 hours and up to 3 days.

Stir and turn several times a day.

When ready to serve, drain the sauce from the seafood and serve cold on a platter with toothpicks.

My mother-in-law, Bobbie, was a great cook and original "home chef." She had a wonderful instinct regarding flavor combinations and was able to use this talent to make fabulous, sometimes unusual, meals. I married into the family at the age of 15 and was completely terrified to cook for her. Most of the cooking skills that my daughters and I acquired are because of Bobbie. She forced me to face my fears, pull out the cookbooks, pots and pans and jump into the broth. I thank her for being such a great role model.

Val Wilson, Atria El Camino Gardens Engage Life volunteer

Mémère's Famous Beef Soup

Prep Time: 30 minutes | Cook Time: 4 hours | Servings: 6

Ingredients:

2 lbs. beef, cut up

1 onion, chopped

2 stalks of celery, chopped

4 carrots, sliced

2 c. tomato sauce

1 c. water

salt and pepper to taste

Preparation:

Brown the beef on all sides in a Dutch oven.

Combine remaining ingredients and pour over beef.

Simmer for at least 4 hours on low heat.

Enjoy with homemade bread or rolls.

Mémère's famous beef soup recipe was passed down from my grandmother, Alexina Gallant, who created it in the late 1800s! We called her "Mémère," which is French for grandmother. She emigrated from Canada to Sanford, Maine. We had to stay behind, but were able to visit often. Mémère kept us comfortable and well-fed with this soup when we visited. We had limited means and this recipe was affordable to make and easy to double and triple.

Juliette Scarponi, Atria Kennebunk resident

Mini Tomato-Pesto Tarts

Prep Time: 15 minutes | Cook Time: 12 minutes | Servings: 15 pieces

Ingredients:

⅓ c. mayonnaise
¼ c. mozzarella cheese, shredded
3 tbsp. parmesan cheese, grated
2 tsp. basil pesto
2 plum tomatoes, chopped
15 ready-made phyllo tart shells

Preparation:

Combine mayonnaise, mozzarella cheese, parmesan cheese and basil pesto.

Stir in plum tomatoes.

Spoon filling evenly into tart shells.

Bake at 375°F for 12 minutes.

I got this recipe from a friend when I first moved to Rhode Island. It immediately became a family and party favorite. As an Engage Life Assistant at Atria Harborhill, I introduced the recipe to our cooking club. The club has made these tarts several times and many of our residents enjoy them at Happy Hour. They disappear quickly – make lots!

Suzy Baird, Atria Harborhill Engage Life Assistant

Pimento Cheese

Prep Time: 20 minutes | Servings: 4 – 6

Ingredients:

1 lb. cheddar cheese, grated

1 c. mayonnaise

¼ c. pimentos

Juice of 1 lemon

salt and pepper to taste

Optional:

cayenne pepper

walnuts

garlic

Preparation:

This recipe couldn't get any easier!

Process all ingredients in blender until the mixture reaches a spreadable consistency.

Pimento cheese is a southern staple and can be used in so many different ways: on sandwiches, as a dip, on slices of celery, on crackers, etc. I made this for my friends and family for many years and it was enjoyed by all.

Mary DeLoache, Atria Buckhead resident

Salmon Crepes

Prep Time: 30 minutes | Cook Time: 30 – 40 minutes | Servings: 24

Ingredients:

Crepes:

1 egg

2 c. water

3 c. flour

Filling:

2 (8 oz.) cans red salmon

⅔ c. whipping cream

½ c. Knudsen® cottage cheese

2 tsp. onion, grated

½ c. dill pickle, grated

salt, pepper and paprika to taste

½ pt. whipping cream

8 oz. sharp cheddar cheese, grated

Preparation:

Crepes: Beat eggs and water. Add flour and baking powder. Grease a small frying pan with vegetable oil. Pour mixture into pan enough to cover the bottom with thin layer. Lightly brown each side. Make 24 crepes. Set aside.

Filling: Separate salmon and juice from can, reserving the juice. Remove any bones from salmon. In a bowl, combine salmon, salmon juice, ⅔ cup of whipping cream, cottage cheese, onion, pickles and seasonings for salmon mixture. Add 1 tablespoon of this mixture onto each crepe and fold like an envelope. Place stuffed crepes in a large baking pan. Do not place crepes on top of each other. Add ½ pint whipping cream on top of the crepes and cover with the grated sharp cheddar cheese. Sprinkle with some paprika. Bake for 30 – 40 minutes at 350°F. Serve hot.

The stuffed crepes can be frozen. To bake from frozen state: thaw and then cover with whipping cream and cheese. Follow regular baking directions.

This recipe was created when I hosted two 50th-birthday parties for my husband. For the first party, I ordered the crepes from a caterer and was charged $2.75 per crepe! For the second party, I decided to make the crepes myself. They were so successful, I wanted to share the recipe!

Elfreda Sender, Atria Golden Creek resident

Sausage Corn Soup

Prep Time: 25 minutes | Cook Time: 45 – 60 minutes | Servings: 4

ngredients:

2 c. potatoes, peeled and cubed
1 pkg. smoked sausage
1 (16 oz.) can whole kernel corn, drained
1 (16 oz.) can creamed corn
2 c. milk

Preparation:

In a medium pot, add 6 cups of water.

Add potatoes and boil until tender.

Slice sausage and brown in a frying pan.

Add sausage, corn and milk to the pot.

Cook until warm (but not to boiling) and then serve.

I received this recipe from a family member and didn't find the title appetizing. I held onto it for 20 years before finally deciding to try it. I served it to my sister-in-law, and she said it was incredible. I then realized how good it was and am kicking myself for not trying it earlier. I made it all the time for supper after that.

Pat Feldman, Atria Eastlake Terrace resident

Spanish Garbanzo Bean Soup

Prep Time: 20 minutes | Cook Time: 2 – 3 hours | Servings: 10 – 12

Ingredients:

1 large onion, diced

2 tbsp. vegetable oil

15 oz. can garbanzo beans, drained

2 – 4 medium potatoes, roughly diced

½ lb. ham, diced

1 tsp. salt

1 tsp. curry powder

dash of pepper

Preparation:

Use a 3-quart sauce pan. Heat onion in oil until transparent.

Add beans, potatoes and ham. Cover with water and add salt, curry powder and pepper.

Simmer slowly, covered, for 2 – 3 hours.

This garbanzo bean soup was something we loved. My mom and dad made it after holidays, like Christmas or Easter, when we usually had leftover ham. The origins of this recipe are from soups served in the 1930s Depression-era food lines. In those soups, they would have added bones for flavor instead of ham, and the garbanzo beans would have served as the major source of protein.

Story submitted by Debbie Mundy, pictured here with her mother, Atria Sutton resident Vivian Black

Entrées

The hearty weekday supper that keeps the family fed and happy.
The crowning centerpiece of a holiday dinner that elicits a chorus
of oohs, ahhs and mmms. The roast that helped your mother win
your father's heart.

Aline's Lobster Mac and Cheese

Prep Time: 20 minutes | Cook Time: 25 minutes | Servings: 6 – 8

Ingredients:

- 2 large lobsters (you can use frozen, cooked lobster)
- 1 lb. elbow macaroni
- 3 tbsp. butter
- 3 tbsp. flour
- 1 c. whole milk
- 1 c. heavy cream
- salt and pepper to taste
- 2 c. sharp cheddar cheese, shredded
- 1 c. bread crumbs (any, but I use panko)

Preparation:

Fill large pot with water and bring to a boil. Add the lobster and cook until the lobster turns red. Remove the lobster from the pot and let cool. Then, cut lobster into bite-sized pieces and set aside.

Cook the macaroni in boiling water until firm, about 10 – 11 minutes. Drain and set aside.

In a deep pan, melt the butter over medium heat. Add the flour to make a roux. Stir to remove any lumps. Pour in the milk and heavy cream and cook until thick and smooth. Season with salt and pepper to taste. Add the cheese and stir until melted. Add the cooked macaroni and lobster meat and stir.

Transfer all to a 2-quart casserole dish. Sprinkle bread crumbs on top. Bake in a preheated oven at 350°F for 25 minutes or until the edges are bubbly.

This is the first recipe my mother, Aline, ever learned to make as a child. It has been in our family ever since. When I was a little girl, she taught me how to make it, and I always enjoy sharing this dish with others. My husband and son can't get enough of it!

Deborah Martin, Atria Maplewood Place Engage Life Director

Barbecue Sauce

Cook Time: 4 – 5 hours | Makes: 1 – 1 ½ gallons

Ingredients:

7 ½ c. water

2 tsp. cayenne pepper

½ c. onion, minced

1 ½ c. honey

2 ½ c. Jack Daniel's® whiskey

½ c. white vinegar

2 c. molasses

½ c. garlic, minced

1 tsp. onion powder

3 c. ketchup

1 c. white sugar

1 tsp. salt

¼ c. Lawry's® seasoning

¾ c. vegetable oil

4 c. tomato paste

1 c. raspberry preserves

¾ c. Worcestershire sauce

6 c. brown sugar

½ tsp. black pepper

1 tbsp. paprika

2 cans Coors® beer

1 c. mustard

¼ c. barbecue spice

15 oz. can Campbell's® tomato soup

Preparation:

Combine all of the ingredients in a large mixing bowl or stock pot. Using a hand mixer, food processor or blender, puree until smooth.

In a large stock pot, simmer for 4 – 5 hours, stirring occasionally.

Serve over ribs, pork chops or chicken.

When I was six years old, my grandmother started to teach me to cook. I had always enjoyed making strange concoctions, but learning how to really cook helped distract me from my mother's battle with breast cancer. One 4th of July, my uncle, who considered himself an expert chef, was in the kitchen making barbecue sauce for our celebration. He got into an argument with other family members about how it tasted. I spoke up and said I could make it; of course everyone laughed. They didn't know about my secret training with my grandmother. It was decided there would be a cooking contest between my uncle, age 30, and me, age 7. Family members ran to the store to grab supplies and the house was soon filled with laughter and dirty dishes, which the loser had to wash. My grandmother just sat quietly at the kitchen table, not saying a word about our secret. The end of the story is very simple: the 7-year-old didn't have to do the dishes and a proud grandma kept our secret for many years. I've enjoyed cooking throughout my life…thanks Grandma!

Glen Wise, Atria Collwood Director of Culinary Services

Bea's Oyster and Cheese Casserole

Prep Time: 10 minutes | Cook Time: 20 minutes | Servings: 4

Ingredients:

1 c. bread crumbs, dry

1 pt. oysters or 1 lb. sea scallops

8 oz. (approx. 2 c.) cheddar cheese, grated

½ tsp. salt

dash of cayenne pepper

1 c. milk (or use less and add a touch of vermouth)

dash of curry (if desired)

Preparation:

Cover bottom of buttered casserole dish (1 qt. size) with a layer of bread crumbs. Cover with a layer of oysters or sea scallops. Add a layer of cheese. Repeat layers until ingredients are used up, and cover the top with cheese and a thin sprinkle of crumbs.

Mix salt, cayenne, curry and milk/vermouth. Make a small hole in the center with a spoon and pour in the liquid. Dot with butter.

Bake at 450°F for 20 minutes.

My mom was a fabulous cook. When I got married, she put together a book of family specialties which she called Marmalade Kitchen because she and my dad made batches of marmalade for many years. This is a recipe from that book. This one is from Aunt Bea, who lived in Plymouth, Massachusetts and was a wonderful cook. It's a family favorite.

Story submitted by Anne Bouchard, daughter of Atria Buckhead resident Joan Midgley, pictured here

Beer-Braised Lamb Shanks

Prep Time: 10 minutes | Cook Time: 1 ½ hours | Servings: 4

Ingredients:

2 lamb shanks
olive oil
6 garlic cloves, chopped
1 medium onion, chopped
salt and pepper to taste
3 cans beer

Preparation:

Brown lamb shanks over medium-high heat in olive oil.

Add garlic, onions, salt and pepper to taste.

After shanks are browned, deglaze with 3 cans of beer and lower heat to a simmer for an hour or until shanks are tender.

Serve lamb with your favorite potato, rice, or noodle and vegetable, and don't forget the San Francisco sourdough bread!

I traveled all over the country with my husband, Marion, who was in the military for 20 years as a Master Sergeant and Food Inspector. We spent time in Fort Lewis, Washington, San Francisco, California and New Orleans, Louisiana. While stationed in San Francisco, we made some really good friends, so when my husband finally retired from the military, we chose to settle in the Bay Area. He found a job there and we enjoyed living in Pacifica. We entertained Marion's new boss at our home by preparing his favorite meal, lamb shanks. Everyone loved this dish and it became a staple of get-togethers in our home.

June Phinney, Atria Sunnyvale resident

Cabbage Rolls

Cook Time: 1 hour | Servings: 4

Ingredients:

- 1 lb. ground meat
- 1 c. onions, white or yellow
- 1 garlic clove, chopped
- 1 c. bell peppers, diced
- cabbage leaves
- toothpicks

Preparation:

Brown ground meat. Sauté onions, garlic and bell pepper until tender, then combine with ground meat.

Stuff cabbage leaves with mixture and secure with toothpicks.

Bake at 350°F for 30 – 45 minutes in a 9"x 13" baking dish.

As a young bride, I first cooked fried pork chops, canned butter beans and sliced tomatoes. After about two weeks, we were looking for something else! I asked a friend for her recipe for cabbage rolls. She gave me this recipe, and I did as instructed. Imagine my surprise when I checked to see how it was coming. The cabbage leaves were merrily bubbling away from the meat – what a mess! She forgot to tell me to secure the cabbage with toothpicks. It's a mistake I never made again.

Katherine Thompson, Atria Collier Park resident

Charlie's Special Meatloaf

Prep Time: 15 minutes | Cook Time: 25 – 30 minutes | Servings: 8

Ingredients:

10 oz. bag spinach, frozen and chopped
1 lb. ground beef
1 c. bread crumbs
2 tbsp. fresh parsley, chopped
2 eggs
1 small onion, chopped
4 tbsp. ketchup
½ c. red wine
¼ c. parmesan cheese, grated (optional)

Preparation:

Defrost the spinach and reserve the water. Once defrosted, squeeze spinach dry and reserve that water, too.

In a large bowl, mix all of the ingredients. If desired, use 2 – 3 tablespoons of the reserved spinach water to make meatloaf more moist.

Shape into a loaf in your favorite pan.

Bake in oven at 450°F for 25 – 30 minutes.

Let sit before serving.

This is the only dish I ever made. For most of my life, I kept the recipe a secret, never sharing it with anyone – not even my wife, Frances! Anytime I made this meatloaf, I'd immediately hide the recipe back in my home office desk. Everyone in the family loved this meal and tried very hard to get me to share the ingredients with them. I never would do it. After moving to Atria Bay Shore, my family finally found my secret hiding place. Since the secret's out, you might as well know, too, so I've given my permission to include it in this recipe book for all to enjoy.

Charles Gulotta, Atria Bay Shore resident

Chicken and Dumplings

Prep Time: 30 minutes | Cook Time: 1 ½ hours | Servings: 4 – 5

Ingredients:

Chicken:

(4 – 5 lbs.) roasting chicken

salt and pepper to taste

Dumplings:

½ c. flour

2 tsp. baking powder

1 tsp. salt

¾ c. water

Preparation:

Chicken: Cut chicken into 8 pieces. Cover with cold water and boil with salt and pepper to taste.

Remove chicken pieces, set aside and keep warm.

Dumplings: Combine flour, baking powder and salt with ¾ cup of the warm water and mix into a smooth dough. Roll out into ½" thickness. Cut into oblong dumplings, 1 ½" x 3."

Drop dumpling dough into the rest of the boiling broth for about 5 minutes or until done.

Serve dumplings with the chicken pieces.

I am 90 years old. I watched my grandma make these dumplings as a child. My mother made them and this was always a favorite of mine. My mother also made noodles, and the family would vote if we were having noodles or dumplings. I would always vote for dumplings!

My mother used her hands to measure her ingredients. My granddaughter, when she was six years old, asked for the recipe. My mother had to measure the amounts she previously measured with her hands. This is how we have this recipe to pass along to you.

Catherine Murphy, Atria Covell Gardens resident

Chicken and Rice Casserole

Prep Time: 15 minutes | Cook Time: 1 hour | Servings: 8 – 10

Ingredients:

1 stick margarine
2 c. rice, uncooked
1 (2 oz.) pkg. Lipton® onion soup mix
1 c. water, hot
2 lbs. chicken tenders
10 oz. cream of mushroom soup
salt and pepper to taste
1 bay leaf

Preparation:

Melt margarine and coat bottom of 9"x 13" baking dish.

Add 2 cups rice.

Combine 1 package of onion soup mix and 1 cup of hot water, then pour over rice.

Place chicken tenders over rice. Salt and pepper chicken to taste.

Combine cream of mushroom soup and 1 cup of hot water, then pour over chicken.

Add 2 cups of water, bay leaf and bake at 375°F for 1 hour.

Remove bay leaf after cooking.

My son, Doug, had just graduated from Rice University and gotten his first apartment, so I sent him this easy recipe so he could cook it with no trouble. He tried to make it one day and I got a call from him. He said, "Mom, there's too much stuff in it and it won't fit in a pan." I said, "Well, you just got your engineering degree, you figure it out!" A larger pan solved the whole problem.

Jestene Ashcraft, Atria Cypresswood resident

Coquilles St. Jacques

Prep Time: 10 minutes | Cook Time: 40 minutes | Servings: 8

Ingredients:

- 1 bay leaf
- 1/4 tsp. thyme
- salt and pepper to taste
- 2 c. scallops, fresh or frozen
- 1/2 lb. mushrooms, sliced
- 1 small onion, chopped
- 1 tbsp. parsley or chives, chopped
- 5 tbsp. butter
- 1/2 c. dry wine, white
- 2 tbsp. flour
- 2 tbsp. heavy cream
- 1 egg yolk
- bread crumbs, buttered

Preparation:

Bring 3 cups of water to boil with bay leaf, thyme, salt and pepper. Add washed and drained scallops. Poach for about 10 minutes or until tender. Remove the scallops, strain and reserve the poaching liquid.

In a separate pan, sauté mushrooms, onions and parsley in 2 tablespoons of butter. Add white wine and simmer another 10 minutes.

In another pan, melt 2 tablespoons of butter. Add flour and blend well, making a roux. Gradually add 1 cup of poaching liquid and whisk until thick and smooth. In a separate bowl, beat together cream and egg yolk. Temper the cream and egg mixture by adding a small amount of the hot roux and poaching liquid from the pan, and stir vigorously to keep eggs from scrambling. Repeat with a little more hot liquid, if necessary, to bring the cream and egg mixture up to the same temperature as what is in the pan. Add the cream and egg mixture to the pan and gradually add the remaining 2 cups of poaching liquid while stirring constantly.

Combine sauce with mushroom mixture and scallops. Fill ramekins and sprinkle with buttered crumbs. Dot with butter and place in the oven until the crumbs turn golden brown.

I lived in France, near Paris, for four years. While there, I took every opportunity afforded me, including how to make some French specialty dishes, Coquilles St. Jacques being one of them. Upon returning to the States, I entertained often and my favorite menu was this dish for a luncheon served with crisp French bread and cheese, with pots de crème for dessert. Instead of ramekins, I served this dish in sea shells from Normandy beach, gathered and given to me from my French friends.

Juanita Edmondson, Atria Valley Manor resident

Cornish Pasties

Prep Time: 30 minutes | Cook Time: 1 hour | Servings: 4

Ingredients:

Pastry:

2 c. all-purpose flour

1 tsp. salt

⅔ c. + 2 tbsp. cold shortening

4 – 5 tbsp. cold water

Filling:

1 lb. top sirloin, ½" cubes

1 c. large red or Yukon Gold potatoes, cooked, peeled and cubed

¼ c. yellow onion, minced (optional)

4 slices bacon, cooked and crumbled

salt and pepper to taste

4 tsp. butter, cut in small pieces

Preparation:

Pastry: Combine flour and salt in medium bowl. Cut in shortening with pastry blender until pea-sized. Gradually toss in cold water, using a fork to blend until all flour is moistened. Gather dough into a ball, then divide in two. Flatten each ball into a disc. Wrap in plastic wrap and chill for 30 minutes. After chilling, roll out pastry; cut into six – 7" rounds.

Filling: Cover half of the pastry (leaving ½" border) with meat, potatoes, onions and bacon. Season with salt and pepper. Dot with butter and sprinkle lightly with water. Fold one half of pastry over the other. Crimp and seal edges. Cut small slit on top. Place pasties on ungreased baking sheet.

Bake at 350°F for 1 hour.

Around 1876, this recipe was brought to the United States by my grandparents, William and Annie Perryman, from Cornwall, England. My grandfather was a miner who immigrated to California with three brothers. He settled in Sierra City, where my mother was born. The Cornish miners took hot pasties (pronounced *pass-ty*) to work in their lunch buckets, and their kids took them to school. There were a number of other immigrants from Ireland, Germany and Italy, so the Cornish kids would trade pasties for Italian raviolis or German sausage. My sister and I were raised eating Cornish pasty. So were our children, and now our grandchildren are being raised correctly, too!

Bill Green, Atria El Camino Gardens resident

Crock-Pot Pheasant

Prep Time: 30 minutes | Cook Time: 12 – 16 hours | Servings: 10 – 12

Ingredients:

1 wild pheasant breast, cleaned

½ c. celery, chopped

lettuce (enough to line bottom of crock pot)

½ c. onion, diced

½ c. carrots, diced

1 c. chicken broth

1 c. raw wild rice, rinsed

salt and pepper to taste

Preparation:

Wash and dry pheasant breast in cold water.

Line bottom of Crock-Pot® with lettuce. Add celery on top of lettuce. Add enough water to moisten. Place pheasant breast on top and cover pot. Cook on low heat for 6 – 8 hours or overnight.

Remove meat. Discard greens and fill bottom of pot with wild rice. Add chicken broth to cover rice. Next, add carrots and onions. Put meat back on top. Season with salt and pepper. Replace cover. Cook additional 6 – 8 hours and serve. Check occasionally to see if rice is dry: if so, add water in ½ cup intervals as needed.

When we lived in Illinois, one of our neighbors and his friends would hunt for pheasants after dark, usually in a farmer friend's field. Their wives would not let them bring the pheasants to their house, so I would get a knock at the door around 1 a.m., and I knew then it meant filling the tub full of hot water to let them soak for an hour or so before I could pluck them. I saved the feathers for a beautiful bouquet.

Ruth Duncan, Atria Baypoint Village resident

Eggplant Parmigiana

Prep Time: 20 minutes | Cook Time: 50 minutes | Servings: 6

Ingredients:

2 lbs. eggplant (about 2 medium-sized eggplants)

kosher salt, as needed

5 c. fresh breadcrumbs

1 tbsp. dried oregano

1 tbsp. dried thyme

freshly ground black pepper

vegetable oil for frying

all-purpose flour for dredging

6 large eggs

2 tbsp. milk

7 c. marinara sauce

⅔ c. grated parmesan, divided

1 lb. fresh mozzarella, thinly sliced

Preparation:

Cut eggplant into ½" thick round slices. Arrange slices on several baking sheets and sprinkle generously with kosher salt. Set aside at least 1 hour to allow excess water to drain from eggplant.

Rinse eggplant well under cold running water. Blot slices dry with paper towels.

In large bowl, whisk together 1 ½ teaspoons salt, breadcrumbs, oregano, thyme and pepper. Place flour in a shallow plate then set aside. In a medium bowl, whisk eggs and milk together. Dredge each eggplant slice in flour, then dip in egg wash and finally dredge in breadcrumb mixture. Shake off any excess breading and place on baking sheet. In a large skillet, heat ½" of oil over medium heat until reaches 400°F.

Working in small batches, fry eggplant slices, turning once, until golden brown (about 3 minutes per batch). Using tongs, transfer to paper towel-lined baking sheet and season with salt. Repeat with the remaining eggplant.

Preheat oven to 400°F. Cover bottom of a 9"x 13" baking dish with ⅓ of the marinara sauce and arrange half of eggplant over sauce. Cover eggplant with another ⅓ of the sauce. Scatter half of the parmesan and half of the mozzarella over sauced eggplant. Repeat with remaining eggplant, sauce, parmesan and mozzarella. Bake until cheese on top just starts to brown, about 30 minutes.

In 1971, my wife and I asked my father-in-law if we could use his farm property up in Dutchess County, New York to grow vegetables. We grew a large variety without using any chemicals in the soil and sold them to workers in the telephone company where my friend was employed. Each Sunday evening, we loaded up the car with bags of mixed vegetables and dropped them off in Manhattan. We charged $3 a bag for tomatoes, corn, eggplant, zucchini, green and red peppers. Our best was always eggplant, which the soil seemed to love producing. From that we created our favorite dish: eggplant parmigiana!

Arnie Solinsky, Atria Huntington resident

Girl Scouts® Chili

Prep Time: 30 minutes | Cook Time: 2 hours | Servings: 6

Ingredients:

1 c. celery, chopped

1 c. onion, chopped/diced

1 lb. lean hamburger

2 small cans kidney beans

2 cans Campbell's® tomato soup

1 c. white rice, cooked

salt and pepper to taste

2 tbsp. instant coffee (optional)

Preparation:

Sauté the celery and onions. Add the hamburger and cook slowly on low heat.

Add the beans and the soup and simmer for 1 hour.

Add the cooked rice and a little water if the chili is too thick. Salt and pepper to taste.

You can also add 2 tablespoons of instant coffee to rev up the taste.

I earned my Girl Scouts cooking badge with this recipe. As a Girl Scout, we had to prepare dinner. I served this with cole slaw, cornbread and lemon meringue pie. Later, I made this recipe for my family. My daughter was a gymnast and whenever she had an athletic meet, I would make food for the judges and officials. Not a drop of my chili would be left!

Alice "Rosalie" Haddox, Atria Seville resident

Goulash

Prep Time: 30 minutes | Cook Time: 45 minutes | Servings: 4 – 6

Ingredients:

2 c. noodles of choice
1 ½ lbs. ground beef
1 onion, diced
2 tbsp. Lipton® onion soup
1 garlic clove, crushed
1 medium can tomatoes, diced
1 c. celery, diced
¼ c. ketchup
1 tbsp. barbecue sauce

Preparation:

Cook noodles to just slightly underdone, according to package directions. Drain and set aside.

Brown ground beef, diced onions and dry onion soup mix. Drain. Add garlic, diced tomatoes, celery, ketchup and barbecue sauce. Salt and pepper to taste. Add noodles. Stir and simmer for 2 minutes.

Pour into a casserole dish and bake at 350°F for 40 – 45 minutes.

I can remember walking into the house and just the smell of this dish cooking would make me hungry. Now when I cook this, I am reminded of my childhood and my mother in the kitchen fixing this for the family. This dish was always a favorite of everybody and has been handed down from my mother to me. My children and grandchild love this when I make it. I have handed this recipe down to my children now, so that they can make it for themselves.

Nancy Meyers, pictured here with her mother,
Atria Kinghaven resident Effie McGee

Goulash with an Austrian Accent

Prep Time: 20 minutes | Cook Time: 1 ½ hours | Servings: 4

ngredients:

2 tsp. marjoram

1 tsp. caraway seed

1 tsp. lemon rind, finely chopped

1 garlic clove

¾ c. butter

1 tsp. tomato paste

2 lbs. onions, sliced

1 tbsp. paprika

2 lbs. beef (chuck, rump, beef shank or round)

1 ½ c. water, divided

salt to taste

Preparation:

Crush marjoram, caraway seed, lemon rind and garlic together.

Place in large pot and add butter, tomato paste and onions. Sauté until onions are golden. Add paprika and stir for 30 seconds.

Cut beef into 1" cubes. Add to pot. Add 1 cup of water and salt to taste. Cover pot and simmer for 1 ½ hours.

Before removing from the heat, add the remaining ½ cup of water and let it boil up one more time.

This dish brings many memories of our early family before world wars ripped apart the Austrian-Hungarian multi-national culture. Our family traces its Austrian roots to the mid-1300s. As a girl, around 1910, my mother was sent to work in the kitchen of an Austro-Hungarian aristocrat's estate. She brought back many recipes, but we loved to make goulash with an Austrian twist. The goulash can be served with dumplings, noodles, boiled potatoes, rice or spätzle. For the Hungarian touch, my mother would sprinkle it with sliced green and red peppers for garnish. We also used sweet Hungarian paprika. Some German chefs like to roll the beef in paprika, very generously, and then roast it in an oven before adding to a recipe such as this one.

Erika Treutler King, Atria Briarcliff Manor resident

Ham Loaf

Prep Time: 20 minutes | Cook Time: 1 hour | Servings: 12

Ingredients:

Loaf:
1 ¼ lbs. ground ham, smoked
¾ lb. ground pork shoulder
¾ c. cracker crumbs
½ tsp. pepper
2 eggs
¾ c. milk
Glaze:
⅓ c. packed brown sugar
½ c. vinegar
1 tsp. dry mustard

Preparation:

Spray baking dish with non-stick spray.

Mix glaze ingredients and boil for 1 minute.

Combine ham, pork, cracker crumbs, pepper, eggs and milk in large mixing bowl.

Form mixture into loaf and baste with glaze mixture.

Bake at 350°F for 20 minutes and then baste again. Continue baking until loaf is cooked in the middle and reaches internal temperature of 160°F.

For close to 30 years, I spearheaded a ladies group that served fantastic lunches to church members and people in the community. We charged an average of $4 for a meal and gave the proceeds to mission projects sponsored by our church. I fondly remember how successful those Lenten Lunches were.

Ruth Rehn, Atria Newburgh resident

Helen's Stuffed Manicotti

Prep Time: 40 minutes | Cook Time: 35 – 40 minutes | Servings: 8

Ingredients:

1 pkg. Ronzoni® manicotti shells

Filling:

1 ½ c. cottage cheese

½ c. grated romano cheese

½ c. parmesan cheese, grated

1 egg, beaten

¼ tsp. salt

2 tbsp. fresh parsley, chopped

Sauce:

1 lb. lean ground beef

2 tbsp. vegetable or canola oil

½ c. onion, chopped

23 oz. tomato sauce

1 c. water

1 tsp. anise

1 tsp. basil

Preparation:

To make manicotti filling, combine cottage cheese, romano cheese, parmesan cheese, egg, salt and parsley in a bowl.

In a pan, brown ground beef and onion in the oil. Add tomato sauce, water, anise and basil.

Cook shells in salted water; drain and rinse quickly in cold water. Fill shells with cheese mixture.

Pour half of meat sauce in bottom of 9"x 13" glass baking dish. Lay stuffed manicotti on top. Cover with remaining sauce. Sprinkle with parmesan cheese.

Bake at 350°F for 35 – 40 minutes.

Our friend Helen was famous for her delicious stuffed manicotti at our church potlucks! We all tried guessing the ingredients. Yet, she refused to part with the recipe. Even when she entertained close friends in her home, she kept the ingredients a secret. "Some day," she would say, "I'll pass it on to you." Well, only after Helen passed on did we learn the secret to her famous stuffed manicotti. You never would have guessed anise, would you?

Ruth Suttner, Atria Woodbridge resident

Hot Chicken Salad

Prep Time: 30 minutes | Cook Time: 15 minutes | Servings: 8

Ingredients:

⅔ c. green peppers, chopped

1 c. celery, chopped

½ c. onion, chopped

½ c. pimentos, chopped
(in water, not oil)

1 c. mushrooms, sliced

1 c. almonds

4 c. chicken, cooked and diced

1 c. mayonnaise

2 tbsp. butter

1 ½ c. corn flakes

Preparation:

Sauté green peppers, celery, onion, pimentos and mushrooms together in butter until tender. Then add almonds, chicken and mayonnaise and mix.

Place in buttered 9"x 13" baking dish.

Melt 2 tablespoons of butter and toss with cornflakes. Spread buttered corn flakes on top.

Bake at 450°F for 15 minutes. Serve hot.

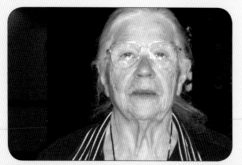

I was a caterer for 35 years. I came up with this recipe all on my own. Over the years, I served many famous people. This particular recipe was one of Walt Disney's and Louis Armstrong's favorite.

June Bell, Atria Golden Creek resident

Iguana Stew

While this dish is not recommended or practical for meal preparation, this story had too much flavor to omit from this collection of culinary memories. Master Sergeant Charles Ohler was captured and held in a Japanese prison camp from July 4, 1944 to September 20, 1945. Atria is proud to have this veteran in our community.

Prep Time: Not long, once you've caught the iguana!
Servings: 5 – 6 hungry soldiers

This is a World War II survival recipe. Fighting in the Philippines, we put this concoction together to supplement our rations. Any other edibles can be added as found, but here's what we used in the field:

1 iguana
fish
wild peppers
water
rice

Since we were out in the field, we had to prepare things as best we could. I wouldn't recommend making iguana stew at home, but back then we had to make do with what we had… start by cutting the top off of a 5-gallon gas can and wash it out thoroughly. Skin and clean iguana and fish. Place all ingredients in gas can and bring to a boil over a fire. Let simmer all day, stirring as needed with rifle.

Chuck Ohler, Atria Manresa resident

Japanese-Style Juicy Chicken Meatballs

Prep Time: 15 minutes | Cook Time: 20 – 30 minutes | Servings: 4 – 5

Ingredients:

Meatballs:

21 oz. chicken, ground

½ c. green onion, finely chopped

½"– 1" piece of ginger root, finely diced

½ c. panko or regular bread crumbs

1 tsp. salt

2 tbsp. sake or white sherry wine

2 tbsp. flour

2 tbsp. vegetable oil

Sauce:

¼ c. soy sauce

¼ c. mirin (Japanese wine sweetener)

¼ c. water

Preparation:

For sauce, mix all the ingredients in a small bowl and set aside.

For the meatballs, mix all ingredients by hand. After mixing ingredients, form small balls by hand. Then, cover with flour and brown in oil in a skillet.

Pour some of the sauce over the browned chicken meatballs and cover for 3 minutes. Afterwards, turn heat on high until the sauce thickens. When the sauce thickens, remove from heat. Place chicken meatballs on a plate and pour rest of sauce on top.

I originally got this idea from a local Japanese recipe book. I never thought it was anything special, but my family loved it. I decided to put my own twist in it, adding a touch of my own spices and new ingredients. My family always looked forward to this meal at a special event. It was their comfort food and made them feel good.

I recall going to Japan to visit my relatives. I made this dish for them. To my surprise, they were very pleased with my interpretation, claiming it was better than the traditional recipe. Their praise made me feel very good about my cooking talents.

Mae Hirasuna, Atria Montego Heights resident

Lasagna

Prep Time: 1 hour | Cook Time: 2 hours | Servings: 8

Ingredients:

Base Sauce:

2 large onions, chopped

8 garlic cloves, minced

6 (28 oz.) cans of imported Italian tomatoes, crushed (I use Luigi Vitelli)

6 tsp. sugar

⅓ c. basil, crushed

pepper to taste

3 lbs. ground meat (optional)

2 c. eggplant, diced (optional)

Lasagna:

23 oz. ricotta cheese

1 egg

1 c. parmesan cheese, grated

2 tbsp. parsley flakes

Barilla® no-boil lasagna noodles

1 lb. mozzarella, shredded

Preparation:

Base Sauce: In large 8-quart pot, sauté onions in just enough olive oil to coat the onions (or the sauce becomes too greasy). Cook on low for about 20 to 30 minutes until onions are translucent. Add garlic and cook until it just starts to turn golden. Add tomatoes, sugar, basil and pepper and bring sauce to a boil. If desired, add sautéed, diced eggplant or browned ground beef to sauce. Lower heat and crack the lid on the pot to allow steam to escape. Stir occasionally to prevent burning. Cook for about an hour.

Lasagna: Mix ricotta with egg, grated parmesan cheese and parsley flakes, set aside. Put layer of sauce on bottom of 9"x 13" pan. Put layer of noodles over sauce. Make layers in the following order: noodles, sauce, dollops of ricotta mixture, shredded mozzarella and grated parmesan cheese. Finish top layer with only mozzarella and grated parmesan cheese.

Cover pan tightly with aluminum foil and bake at 350°F for 1 hour.

Remove from oven. Let rest for 10 minutes before serving.

This is my mom's famous recipe which she handed down to me. The family loves it so much that we have it for Thanksgiving, Christmas and Easter. One year after I took the reins of lasagna maker, I decided that I would make a simpler Thanksgiving and not make the lasagna. The young boys in the family, my mother's grandson and her great nephews, decided that if I wasn't making lasagna, they weren't coming. Guess what we all ate for Thanksgiving? There are always arguments over who gets to take home the leftovers!

Story submitted by Rosalie Barillari, daughter of Atria Tanglewood resident Sarah Civello, pictured here

Mac and Cheese "321"

Prep Time: 20 minutes | Cook Time: 30 minutes | Servings: 10 – 12

Ingredients:

- 1 box ziti (or pasta of choice)
- 3 (10 ¾ oz.) cans cheddar cheese soup
- ⅔ c. milk
- 10 oz. extra sharp cheddar cheese, shredded
- pepper to taste
- bread crumbs

Preparation:

Cook pasta, drain and set aside.

On top of stove, pour cream of cheddar soup into a pot. Add milk and cheese. Stir until melted. Put pasta in a 9"x 13" pan and pour the mixture over the pasta. Top with bread crumbs.

Cover pan with aluminum foil. Bake in oven at 350°F for 25 minutes.

Remove foil for the last 5 minutes of baking to brown bread crumbs.

This has been in my family for quite some time and if I ask what to bring to any gathering, everybody always asks for the mac and cheese "321." It makes a great supper for the family, too.

This macaroni and cheese recipe is so easy to make, delicious and everyone loves it. It is called mac and cheese "321" because of the ingredients that go into making it: 3 cans of soup, 2 cans worth of milk and 1 block of cheese.

Trudy Camerio, Atria Woodbriar receptionist

Meatloaf
(with Easy Gluten-Free Modification)

Prep Time: 15 minutes | Cook Time: 2 hours | Servings: 6 – 8

Ingredients:

¼ c. onion, chopped

2 tsp. parsley

1 – 2 slices bread, cubed
(can substitute gluten-free bread)

⅓ c. celery, finely chopped
(include celery tops for added flavor)

1 c. corn flakes

¾ c. milk

2 lbs. 85% ground meat

2 eggs, whipped

¼ c. ketchup

1 tsp. mustard

1 tsp. brown sugar

salt and pepper to taste

Preparation:

Soak onion, parsley, bread, celery and corn flakes in milk.

While soaking, mix together meat, egg, ketchup, mustard, brown sugar, salt and pepper. Combine all ingredients together and form into oval shape.

Pour a little water over meatloaf. Spread ketchup on top.

Cover with foil and bake at 350°F for 1 hour, 45 minutes.

Remove foil and continue baking for an additional 15 minutes.

Let stand several minutes to solidify before cutting.

Moist and delicious – my signature dish. When I was diagnosed with Celiac disease, this was an easy recipe to modify to ensure it was wheat-free and Celiac-safe. Our family's favorite comfort food meal: meatloaf, scalloped potatoes (thickened with cornstarch) and any vegetable. Try it!

Virginia (Freeman) Pletcher, Atria Penfield resident

Mom's Marinara Sauce and Meatballs

Prep Time: 20 minutes | Cook Time: 1 ½ hours | Servings: 6 – 8

Ingredients:

Sauce:

4 (28 oz.) canned tomatoes, or 5 c. fresh tomatoes

3 garlic cloves, minced

6 leaves basil, chopped

¼ tsp. ground fennel

olive oil

salt and pepper to taste

Meatballs:

1 ½ lbs. ground beef and veal, combined

3 eggs

3 garlic cloves, chopped

½ c. seasoned bread crumbs

3 slices bread, soaked in milk (excess squeezed out)

½ c. grated parmesan cheese

¼ c. parsley, chopped

pinch of ground fennel

pinch of pepper

Preparation:

Sauce: Blend tomatoes. If using fresh tomatoes, only add half of the juice they form, otherwise the sauce will be too thin.

Cover bottom of large pot with olive oil. Add garlic and sauté until it starts to brown. Add the rest of the sauce ingredients and bring to a boil.

Reduce to simmer and cook for 1 to 1 ½ hours. Skim off foam as it forms.

Meatballs: Combine ground beef and veal in bowl and mix together. In a separate bowl, mix together the remaining ingredients until well blended. Combine with meat and roll into balls.

Broil on greased cookie sheet or broiler pan until nicely browned on all sides. Add to marinara sauce.

As long as I can remember, I made this marinara sauce with meatballs every Sunday. It was one of those things my family could always count on. It didn't matter how many people showed up to eat, I made sure that there was always enough pasta with marinara and meatballs to go around. I don't cook anymore, but the recipe is on paper and has been shared with all family members. Now I'm sharing it with you. Best meatballs you will ever eat – enjoy!

Virginia Occhipinti, Atria Chateau Gardens resident

"More"

Prep Time: 15 minutes | Cook Time: 1 hour | Servings: 8

ngredients:

2 lbs. beef, ground

1 lb. pork sausage

1 medium onion, chopped

1 large bell pepper, chopped

3 cans tomato soup

1 can pitted ripe olives

1 small jar pimentos

1 can shoepeg corn

1 can green peas

12 oz. spaghetti

grated cheese (your choice)

Preparation:

Brown the beef and sausage. Drain off the fat and set the browned meat aside.

Sauté the onion and green pepper. Combine with tomato soup, olives, pimentos, corn and peas. Add the meat and let everything cook together on low heat for about 30 minutes.

Cook the spaghetti according to package directions.

In a 9"x 13" pan, layer pasta and meat mixture, beginning and ending with meat. Top with grated cheese.

Bake at 350°F for 30 minutes.

This is our family's favorite recipe. We would sit around and say, "I want more!" – thus the recipe's name! It's really convenient and is a great make-ahead dish for a crowd. You can make it a day in advance and refrigerate. It's also great as leftovers!

Auston Gray, Atria Forest Lake resident

New England Corned Beef and Cabbage

Prep Time: 1 day | Cook Time: 4 – 5 hours | Servings: 6 – 8

Ingredients:

1 (3 lb.) corned beef with seasoning packet
1 lb. white potatoes
4 – 5 large carrots
2 large onions
1 rutabaga
1 head cabbage

Preparation:

Put corned beef in a large pot with plenty of water and add package of seasoning.

Cook corned beef until it's tender. Take out of pot and put aside to cool, then refrigerate.

Take the juice from the big pot and drain it into a large bowl. Refrigerate overnight.

The next day, skim off all the fat from the broth. Put the broth in the big pot with the cold corned beef. Add peeled whole potatoes, carrots cut in half, onions whole, sliced rutabaga and big chunks of cabbage.

Cook the vegetables until tender. Serve on a plate with a deep lip, and pour extra broth from the pot onto meat and vegetables, if desired.

I was born in New Hampshire on December 8, 1920 – I'm a real New England Yankee! I love my Irish heritage and am fond of its traditional food, song and dance. I always made this dish to serve on St. Patrick's Day. May you enjoy the recipe – you will find that once you try it, you'll never make any other kind of corned beef and cabbage. It's a wonderful dish, enjoy!

Viola Kilpatrick, Atria Chandler Villas resident

Patti's Dance Teacher Special

Prep Time: 5 minutes | Cook Time: 25 minutes | Servings: 4

Ingredients:

1 lb. penne

1 bag spinach, frozen or fresh

1 bag corn, frozen or fresh

½ lb. jumbo shrimp, frozen

1 jar marinara sauce (optional)

2 tsp. chopped garlic

5 – 7 tbsp. olive oil

salt to taste

butter to taste (optional)

Preparation:

Bring a large pot of heavily salted water to a boil.

While waiting, heat 3 tablespoons of olive oil in large sauté pan and add garlic. Gently sauté until golden. Add frozen shrimp and marinara sauce, heating through over medium-low heat. If pan or ingredients are drying out, add another tablespoon or two of olive oil.

Add pasta to boiling water and cook until al dente. Add frozen vegetables to pasta and return to boil for several minutes.

Drain pasta and vegetables. Return to pot; add shrimp, sauce, 2 more tablespoons of olive oil (or butter if desired) and salt to taste.

Mix together and serve!

This recipe is a result of our very busy schedules. Work, raising the kids and Patti's long ballet rehearsal weekends never left much time or desire for grocery shopping in our household. So one tired night, Patti threw together these non-perishables and came up with quite a dish. It is one we enjoy on nights where we just want to relax and watch some television. Inexpensive and easy to make, this pasta recipe is perfect for families on the go. If it seems to need a "little something," just add some butter – a favorite topping of Patti's mother.

John and Patti Moore, Atria Senior Living Chief Executive Officer and his wife

Phoenixville's Favorite Hoagie

Prep Time: 5 minutes | Servings: 1 – 2

Ingredients:

6" or 12" soft roll
2 tbsp. olive oil
shredded lettuce
2 – 4 slices of provolone cheese
sliced ham
sliced salami
tomatoes, sliced
onions, sliced
hot or sweet peppers
salt
pepper
oregano

Preparation:

Slice soft roll down middle to create a sandwich bun.

Apply olive oil to the inside.

Add lettuce, cheese, ham and cooked salami. Top with tomatoes, onions and peppers.

Season with salt, pepper and oregano.

I owned Hirsch's Grocery for 59 years in Phoenixville, Pennsylvania. Every day, I would open the store at 6 a.m., prepare hot coffee and get the daily newspaper ready for all my patrons. My hoagies were very popular around Phoenixville. Oftentimes, I'd have a line clear out the door. Although my recipe is very simple and classic American, I'm thrilled to share it with you. But I insist that it be built in this exact order!

Freda Hirsch, Atria Woodbridge Place resident

Pon Haus (Scrapple)

Prep Time: 30 minutes | Cook Time: 3 hours | Servings: 12 – 15 servings

Ingredients:

Meat:
1 (3 lb.) bone-in pork butt, trimmed of fat
4 qt. water
salt and pepper to taste

Loaf:
2 ½ c. reserved stock
2 tsp. sage, rubbed
1 ½ tsp. thyme, dried
1 tsp. savory, ground
⅛ tsp. ground allspice
⅛ tsp. ground nutmeg
⅛ tsp. ground clove
3 c. cornmeal

Preparation:

Bring pork to a boil in an 8-quart pot. Reduce heat and add a little salt and pepper. Cover and simmer about 2 hours, until the meat is tender. Remove the meat and reserve the stock. When the meat has cooled, remove any fat and bones. Chop the meat finely and set aside.

Strain stock into a 5-quart pot. Add sage, thyme, savory, allspice, nutmeg and clove. Bring to a boil. Stirring briskly, add cornmeal. Reduce heat to simmer and continue stirring for about 15 minutes, until mixture is nearly thick enough for the spoon to stand on its own.

Add the meat to the pot. Adjust seasoning if needed. Line two 9"x 5" loaf pans with wax paper and pour the cooked mixture evenly into them. Refrigerate overnight.

Next day, remove from refrigerator and slice into ½" thick pieces and brown each side in a buttered or oiled skillet. If it's not sufficiently thick, you can coat the slice with flour before browning. Serve with maple syrup, apple butter or ketchup.

My father started farming for his mother at the age of 15, after his father died. He and

my mother were married in 1915. It was in the late 1920s or early 1930s when a salesman for *Household* magazine came by. My mother was away, but my sister and I were sure she'd want to renew her subscription. The problem was that we didn't have any money. We ended up trading him two live chickens!

Years later, I not only subscribed to the magazine, I also ordered their cookbook. I found in there a wonderful recipe for pon haus, a Pennsylvania Dutch dish that is also called "scrapple." It is said that they use all parts of the pig except the squeal.

Inez Savage, Atria Bell Court Gardens resident

Pot Roast

Prep Time: 15 minutes | Cook Time: 4 hours | Servings: 8

Ingredients:

6 lb. pot roast
2 tbsp. ground ginger
2 tbsp. garlic powder
2 – 3 onions, sliced or chopped
1 tbsp. cranberry sauce

Preparation:

Rub roast with ground ginger and garlic powder.

Place in pot with sliced or chopped onions.

Cook on stove top or in Crock-Pot,® covered, on very low heat for about 4 hours.

At the last ½ hour of cooking, mix the cranberry sauce with the pan juices and baste the roast.

The trick in this dish is the cranberry sauce. It brings all the flavors together. All ingredient amounts can be tailored to your liking – I never measured the amounts until now!

Jean Schmetterling, Atria South Setauket resident

Potted Chicken

Prep Time: 30 minutes | Cook Time: 1 ½ hours | Servings: 4 – 6

Ingredients:

1 large onion
3 carrots
2 stalks of celery
2 – 3 white potatoes
2 c. water
1 (3 lb.) chicken
parsley to taste

Preparation:

Cut the onion into small pieces. Slice the carrots and celery. Cut the potatoes into small pieces. Put the vegetables in a large pot, then add 2 cups of water. Start cooking over low heat.

Cut up the chicken into quarters, then add to pot. If needed, add enough water to cover chicken.

Cook the chicken and vegetables for 1 ½ hours. Check to be sure the chicken is done. If not done, cook another 15 minutes, constantly checking until done.

Strain and serve chicken with vegetables. Garnish with parsley.

This recipe started in the early 1900s with my grandmother. When my mother got married, she learned to make this chicken for Sabbath dinner. I helped my mother prepare the chicken as a young girl. Then, when I grew up and got married, this chicken became our Sabbath dinner. Our daughters grew up eating this chicken and each learned how to prepare it. As they got married and established their own homes, it became their Sabbath dinner, too! We now have three granddaughters who prepare this chicken. And so it goes, from generation to generation.

Annette Lipshitz, Atria Lynbrook resident

Roast Beef and Yorkshire Pudding

Prep Time: 10 minutes | Cook Time: 2 hours | Servings: 6 – 8

Ingredients:

Roast:
2 ½ – 3 lb. boneless rump roast
4 – 6 oz. suet
1 ½ c. onion, chopped
4 tbsp. flour
2 c. cold water
Pudding:
2 eggs, beaten
1 c. milk
1 c. flour
1 tsp. salt

Preparation:

Roast Beef: In a large Dutch oven, cook down the suet over medium heat to yield grease for browning the roast. Brown meat well on all sides. After meat is evenly browned, add 1 tablespoon water and the chopped onion. Cover with lid and cook on low heat for 30 minutes per pound of meat. Remove meat from pan.

Cook the remaining liquid down until all of the water is gone and there is about ½ cup of grease remaining in the pan. Grease should appear almost black. Remove any pieces of suet, and all but ¼ cup of grease. Add 4 tablespoons flour to grease to make a paste in bottom of pan. Slowly stir in 2 cups cold water while cooking over medium heat until gravy is thickened and all black bits from cooked onion and suet are dissolved in gravy.

Pudding: Mix eggs, milk, flour and salt into a batter. Pour 2 tablespoons of grease into a 9"x 13" cake pan and bake in a preheated oven at 375°F. When grease is smoking hot, take pan out and pour batter into the pan. Place pan back in oven and bake for 25 – 30 minutes until pudding is puffed up and a nice brown color.

My mother made the same meal for Sunday dinner for as long as I can remember. She enjoyed setting a beautiful table and on Sundays, she would use her lace table cloth, her china dishes, a beautiful centerpiece and candles. She was a working mother and Sunday was the only day she could take time to make a special meal for her family. The house would fill with the smell of roast beef early in the afternoon as she browned the meat and then simmered the roast for hours. The dark gravy was her specialty. The secret to her gravy is in her recipe. We put the tasty, dark gravy on mashed potatoes and her Yorkshire pudding. I am sure this recipe was handed down to my mother by my Grandmother Anderson, because Yorkshire pudding was a dish my grandfather ate as a boy in Scotland.

Margaret Emerick, Atria Tamalpais Creek Engage Life Director

Romanian/Hungarian Stuffed Cabbage

Prep Time: 40 minutes | Cook Time: 2 hours | Servings: 2 – 3

Ingredients:

- 1 large cabbage
- 2 lbs. ground beef
- 1 medium onion, finely chopped
- 1 c. Minute® Rice
- 1 c. raisins
- 1 egg, beaten
- salt and pepper to taste

Sauce:

- 1 large jar sauerkraut
- 1 (28 oz.) large can crushed tomatoes
- 2 c. tomato sauce
- 4 tbsp. brown sugar (optional)
- water

Preparation:

Parboil cabbage and remove core. Carefully remove leaves and set aside. Combine beef, onion, rice, raisins, egg, salt and pepper in large bowl. Put 2 tablespoons of mixture in the center of each cabbage leaf, fold over, and then roll tightly.

Put the sauerkraut and broken leftover cabbage leaves in the bottom of a large pot.

Place the cabbage rolls carefully in the pot, with the open side down.

Mix tomatoes, tomato sauce and brown sugar, then add to pot.

Simmer for 2 hours. Add water as needed to keep the cabbage rolls moist.

I learned to make stuffed cabbage Romanian-style from a Brooklyn neighbor. Later, after marrying my husband, whose parents were from Hungary, I discovered that Hungarians added sauerkraut to their stuffed cabbage recipes. I combined the two styles and, at the frequent request of my husband and our children, served this dish often. I would chop the mixture in a big wooden bowl. My daughter, Paula, would peel the cabbage leaves. Together, we'd make the cabbage rolls. This dish brings back fond family memories.

Marlene Weiss, Atria Lynbrook resident, pictured here with her daughter, Paula Blum

Steamed Lobster

Prep Time: 20 minutes | Servings: 4 – 6

Ingredients:

4 – 6 lobsters, live
salt

Preparation:

You will need a large stock pot and a steaming rack inside the pot to keep the lobster out of the water. Use a pot big enough so that the lobsters are not crowded.

Put 2" of salted water in the bottom of the pot.

Bring to a rolling boil over high heat.

Add the live lobsters one at a time, cover the pot and start timing (10 minutes per pound of lobster).

Halfway through, lift the lid carefully and shift the lobsters around so they cook evenly. Be careful when you lift the lid, as steam will escape and you don't want to get burned.

My fondest memory is standing around in the kitchen with friends while we steamed lobster. Usually you had friends over for dinner and everything was formal. They came over and were seated in the dining room and you served them. No one saw your kitchen. But when we cooked lobster, we would all stand around and talk while we waited for them to cook. There was a wonderful togetherness on those nights.

Susan Moritz, Atria Inn at Lakewood resident

Stuffed Pork Chops

Prep Time: 30 minutes | Cook Time: 45 minutes | Servings: 4

Ingredients:

1 stick butter, divided

2 ribs celery, finely chopped

1 small white onion, finely chopped

5 large mushrooms, finely chopped

¼ c. cilantro, chopped

3 tbsp. garlic salt, divided

1 tsp. poultry seasoning

1 pkg. (6 oz.) Stove Top® stuffing mix
  for pork

4 (2" thick) cut pork chops

¼ c. white wine

Preparation:

Dressing: Sauté ½ stick butter, celery, onion, mushrooms, cilantro, 2 tablespoons garlic salt and poultry seasoning until onions have softened. Add the package of pork stuffing and lightly stir together. Take off stove, cover, and let it stand for 10 minutes.

Pork Chops: Take paring knife and cut lengthwise into each chop to make a pocket, being careful not to cut all the way through. Stuff the pork chops with the dressing. Once stuffed, you may want to insert toothpicks around the edge to hold them together. Place stuffed pork chops in a glass baking dish.

In a small sauce pan on low heat, add ½ stick butter, white wine and 1 tablespoon of garlic salt until the butter is melted. Pour this over the pork chops.

Bake dish in oven at 350°F degrees for 45 minutes or until browned well.

I first started making this dish when I got married. My husband loved stuffed turkey and stuffing so much that I started coming up with new things to stuff. So, I created my very own recipe for stuffed pork chops! For decoration, I would place slices of gelled cranberry sauce and parsley on one side of the plate. This dish was on our table every Thursday to celebrate my husband's payday. To this day, all six of my children still request this dish when they come over for special occasions and holidays.

Sharon Butcher, Atria Willow Glen Engage Life Program Instructor

Summer Pasta

Prep Time: 20 minutes | Cook Time: 12 minutes | Servings: 8

Ingredients:

- 1 lb. angel hair pasta
- 6 tomatoes
- fresh basil, about 20 leaves
- 2 tbsp. extra virgin olive oil
- 2 tbsp. fresh chopped garlic
- salt and pepper to taste

Preparation:

Cook angel hair pasta al dente according to package instructions.

Dice the tomatoes and chop the basil.

Mix together the olive oil, tomatoes, garlic and basil, and then toss with the pasta.

Salt and pepper to taste. Serve hot.

I used to make this pasta every summer when the fresh garden tomatoes were most abundant, juicy and flavorful. This recipe has only a small list of ingredients but is big on taste. To be honest, I didn't measure – I just knew how much to add to make the pasta taste good!

Lucille Gondolfo, Atria Greenridge Place resident

Tamale Pie

Prep Time: 20 minutes | Cook Time: 1 hour | Servings: 6

Ingredients:

3 tamales, bought fresh or made, cut up

1 lb. ground beef, browned (season beef with 1 tsp. crushed garlic)

1 (16 oz.) can Dennison's® chili beans

1 (16 oz.) can creamed corn

1 (16 oz.) can whole kernel corn, drained

¾ c. pitted black olives

⅓ lb. Tillamook® cheddar cheese, cubed from block

parmesan cheese, shredded

Preparation:

Coat a 9" x 13" baking dish with cooking spray.

Mix all ingredients, except for parmesan cheese, together in a baking dish.

Top with parmesan cheese.

Bake at 350°F for about an hour.

Shortly after my sister-in-law passed away, I received a recipe book from my niece. To my niece's surprise, she discovered that one of my very own recipes was in that book. My niece found a note in the book that read, "This family favorite was given to my mother by Ruth." My niece received a copy of the recipe from her mother in 1967. Over the years, I've shared the recipe with practically everyone I know and it has become a favorite with a new generation.

Ruth Oberman, Atria Las Posas resident

Therese's Stew

Prep Time: 20 minutes | Cook Time: 2 ½ hours | Servings: 8 – 10

Ingredients:

1 lb. beef, cut into 1" cubes
2 c. water
2 ½ c. potatoes, cubed
1 tbsp. salt
1 tsp. pepper
½ tsp. paprika (optional)
½ tsp. ground allspice (optional)
½ tsp. ground cloves (optional)
1 medium onion, diced
1 lb. carrots, chopped
3 ribs celery, chopped

Preparation:

In a large pot with some oil, brown the meat on all sides. Once meat is browned, add water and bring to boil.

Add cubed potatoes, salt, pepper and optional spices. Cover and simmer for 1 ½ hours.

Cut up onion, carrots and celery. Add vegetables, cover and cook 30 to 40 minutes longer, until vegetables are tender. Adjust salt and pepper as needed and serve.

I used to make a stew from a recipe passed down to me from my grandmother. I added a few secret changes to make the recipe my own though. Oh, how my children used to beg for my stew! It was always a great idea, because it would last all week. It was a real money-saver on our small budget because of the cheap ingredients and the length that one batch would go. Let's just say that when my children asked for this stew, I put on a very large pot!

Therese Mayhew, Atria Woodlands resident

Toothpick Steak

Prep Time: 30 minutes | Cook Time: 1 ½ hours | Servings: 8

ngredients:

2 lbs. steak, round

2 slices bacon (cut in ½" pieces)

cinnamon

toothpicks

1 c. flour

3 tbsp. shortening

salt and pepper

1 c. water

1 can Coca-Cola®

Preparation:

Pound steak on both sides. Cut into strips 2" wide and 4" long.

Place a piece of bacon on each piece of steak. Put a dash of cinnamon on bacon. Roll steak and fasten with toothpicks.

Melt shortening in frying pan. Flour steak and brown in shortening.

Pour water and Coca-Cola over steak and cover tightly.

Bake in oven at 350°F for 1 ½ hours.

What an unusual dish! Rather glamorous – not everyday fare – just the thing to impress my daughter Patti's current beau, who was coming to our house for Sunday dinner after church. My table was set, the toothpick steak was in the oven, and the on-and-off control (which had always worked magically) was set prior to our leaving.

We all trouped in after church, pleasantly greeted by the fragrance of the toothpick steak. However, when we opened the oven, we found the prized dish had overcooked to the point of cremation! The toothpick steak was ruined. We ate the other dishes while Patti blushed. Anyway, here is the recipe. Just check your oven first!

Maggie Wideman, Atria Evergreen Woods resident

Vegetable Lasagna

Prep Time: 25 minutes | Cook Time: 35 – 45 minutes | Servings: 8 – 10

Ingredients:

1 (8 oz.) pkg. lasagna noodles

1 (24 oz.) jar tomato sauce

1 (16 oz.) pkg. frozen mixed vegetables (peas, string beans, zucchini, broccoli, cauliflower, mushrooms)

1 (8 oz.) pkg. mozzarella cheese

4 garlic cloves, minced

fresh basil

dehydrated onion to taste

salt and pepper to taste

Preparation:

Boil the noodles per package directions.

Once cooked, drain liquid.

Layer noodles in a 9"x 13" roasting pan, alternating with tomato sauce, vegetables, cheese, and herbs and spices. Repeat layers as desired.

Top final layer with tomato sauce and cheese.

Bake in oven preheated to 350°F for 35 – 45 minutes or until cooked through.

Our congregation's rabbi asked our food committee to cater his son's bar mitzvah – a tremendous honor. The whole neighborhood was invited. Hundreds were expected. We had to make over 40 pans of lasagna. But how could we boil all those noodles? Then it hit me – boil them in the tomato sauce! Our vegetable lasagna was a total success.

Sylvia Novick, Atria Riverdale resident

Side Dishes

The simplest staple that becomes a masterpiece with the addition of a single ingredient. The potato salad that's welcomed with enthusiasm at the church picnic year after year. The perfect stuffing recipe that happened completely by accident.

Cheese Pudding

Prep Time: 30 minutes | Cook Time: 30 minutes | Servings: 10

ngredients:

White sauce:

2 tbsp. butter

2 tbsp. flour

1 c. milk

salt and pepper to taste

Pudding:

1 ¼ c. soda cracker crumbs, divided

½ lb. American cheese, grated

4 hard-cooked eggs, peeled and grated

1 (7 oz.) can pimentos, grated

2 tbsp. butter, melted

Preparation:

Melt butter in a saucepan over low heat; stir in flour. Stirring constantly, cook for 2 minutes, careful not to let it brown. Gradually stir in milk and continue stirring over low heat until sauce begins to thicken. Season with salt and pepper.

Grease a 9"x 9" casserole dish. Combine ¼ cup of cracker crumbs with melted butter to form the buttered crumb topping. Set aside.

Mix remaining 1 cup crumbs with 2 cups white sauce until the crumbs are well coated.

Begin layering ingredients in the casserole dish, starting with a layer of the crumbs with white sauce. Add a layer of grated cheese, a layer of grated eggs and a layer of grated pimento. Repeat the layers.

Top with buttered cracker crumbs.

Bake at 350°F for about 30 minutes.

This is an old recipe which originated at the Lynn Hotel in Hodgenville, Kentucky. When President Eisenhower visited the Abraham Lincoln Birthplace in the late 1950s, we served him lunch at the Hodgenville Women's Club. He ate two large helpings of this and asked for the recipe to take home.

Jean T. McCubbin, Atria Elizabethtown resident

Duffin's Stuffin'

Prep Time: 30 minutes | Cook Time: 20 minutes | Servings: 10 – 15

Ingredients:

1 large onion, Spanish
1 large red pepper
1 large green pepper
1 lb. sausage, ground
onion powder to taste
garlic powder to taste
2 loaves of white bread
Bell's® seasoning
Kikkoman® soy sauce
olive oil

Preparation:

Chop up onion and peppers very fine. Sauté in olive oil until tender. Set aside.

In another pan, brown the sausage and season with the onion and garlic powder to taste. Drain when done and set aside.

Lightly toast all bread and crumble into a large bowl.

Mix together meat and sautéed vegetables.

Slowly add water until desired consistency is reached. Add the Kikkoman sauce and Bell's seasoning until desired taste is reached. We never measure the sauce or seasoning, but it is a very subtle taste. The texture is more moist than dry.

Bake at 300°F for about 20 minutes, allowing the top to get a little crunchy.

Thanksgiving brings back fond memories for all of us in our house – not just the anticipation of family coming to visit, but especially Dad's stuffing! For most families, the biggest dish of food besides the turkey would be the potatoes...well, in our house it was the stuffing! Here's to you, Dad!

Story submitted by Peggy Rynne, daughter of Atria Kennebunk resident John Duffin, pictured here

Eunice's Corn Soufflé

Prep Time: 15 minutes | Cook Time: 1 hour | Servings: 4 – 6

Ingredients:

1 box of Jiffy® corn muffin mix
1 (14 oz.) can kernel corn, drained
1 (14 oz.) can creamed corn
8 oz. sour cream
3 eggs
salt and pepper to taste

Preparation:

Mix all ingredients together in a large bowl.

Spray baking dish, either round or square, with non-stick spray.

Bake for 1 hour at 350°F.

Remove from oven and enjoy!

This very easy, delicious recipe has made me famous from New York to California. I learned it from my mother and it is one of our family's favorite dishes and something I am always asked to bring to parties. Not to mention, when you are watching your pennies, it is something that is nutritious and not too expensive. That is important when you are feeding a family.

Eunice Cohen, Atria Bay Shore resident

Fried Green Tomatoes

Prep Time: 15 minutes | Cook Time: 30 – 45 minutes | Servings: 4 – 6

Ingredients:

4 – 6 green tomatoes, sliced ¼" thick
salt
pepper
garlic powder (optional)
Cajun seasoning (optional)
1 c. flour
2 eggs, beaten
cornmeal or bread crumbs
bacon grease or vegetable oil

Preparation:

Salt and pepper the tomato slices; dust lightly with flour and optional seasonings.

Dip slices in beaten egg, letting excess drip off, then coat well with cornmeal or bread crumbs.

Fry in hot grease or oil until browned, turning gently (about 3 minutes each side). Keep warm in oven at 200°F to 250°F if frying in batches.

My father-in-law, John, is from Wylam, Alabama. He loves this dish with all his might! His mother was an incredible gardener and cook. Nearly all the food put on the table came from her efforts. This recipe always brings to mind the fond memories John has of his mom.

Story submitted by Romy Vorhees, daughter-in-law of Atria Bayside Landing resident John Aliano, Sr., pictured here

Fried Matzi

Prep Time: 5 minutes | Cook Time: 6 – 8 minutes | Servings: 2 – 4

Ingredients:

- 5 eggs, extra large
- dash of cinnamon
- ½ c. milk
- 4 sheets plain matzoh, broken into pieces
- 3 tbsp. vegetable oil or PAM® (can substitute with rendered chicken fat)
- maple syrup
- sour cream

Preparation:

In mixing bowl, beat eggs. Add dash of cinnamon and milk.

In another bowl, soak the matzoh in warm water for about one minute. Remove and set aside.

Heat oil in large skillet over medium heat. Add matzoh to the egg mixture, tossing gently to coat (making sure not to break up the matzoh too much). Add this to the hot skillet.

Allow matzoh to cook undisturbed for 2 – 3 minutes, or until bottom begins to brown. Turn it over, stirring gently to cook thoroughly and until the other side begins to brown (matzoh will begin to break up at this point and this is normal).

Serve immediately with maple syrup and sour cream.

I learned to make fried matzi when I was a young girl, in my mother's kitchen in Roxbury, Massachusetts. While it is a traditional dish for Passover, we enjoyed it any time of the year. When I had a family of my own, I often made it for my two sons and my daughter. They all make it for their families today and I even have grandsons who are continuing the tradition of making fried matzi in their kitchens, too!

Miriam Wein, Atria Harborhill resident

German Potato Salad

Prep Time: 45 minutes | Servings: 10 – 12

Ingredients:

5 lbs. white potatoes
Marinade:
½ c. water
2 tbsp. vinegar
¼ tsp. salt
2 tsp. oil
Optional:
cooked bacon crumbles
onion, chopped, raw
bacon drippings
hard-boiled eggs

Preparation:

Boil potatoes in skin. Let cool, then peel and slice. Do not cube.

Place in a large mixing bowl. Mix up the marinade ingredients together and pour over potatoes so they are wet but not "swimming." Gently stir, then cover and let sit on the counter, gently turning the potatoes every hour so they marinate evenly.

Close to serving time, add in the optional ingredients if you like. Best if served warm, but not hot.

I spent many years in Germany and this is how you make *real* German potato salad!

Katherine Lotz, Atria Windsor Woods resident

Grandma's Sweet Sliced Pickles

Prep Time: 3 hour | Cook Time: 1 – 2 hours | Servings: 8 – 12 jars

Ingredients:

2 gals. pickling cucumbers
  (4 – 5" long), sliced ⅛" thick

14 small white onions, sliced thin

4 large green peppers, cut small

¾ c. salt, coarse

10 c. sugar (almost 5 lbs.)

1 tbsp. turmeric

1 tsp. clove, ground

1 tsp. celery seed

¼ c. mustard seed

2 qt. vinegar

Preparation:

Combine cucumbers, onions and peppers and mix in coarse salt. Add a weighted cover to compress ingredients. Let sit for 3 hours. Drain well.

Combine dry sugar, turmeric, clove, celery seed and mustard seed. Add vinegar. Combine with drained vegetables.

Place over low heat in 12-quart kettle. Heat through but do not let it come to a boil. Stir often, cooking on low for 1 – 2 hours.

Pack in sterilized jars and seal.

When I was a little girl, we had Sunday dinner at my mom's parent's house. Grandma always served her homemade sweet pickles with dinner. When Grandma stopped making them Mom started to use her recipe. My kids grew up loving their grandma's homemade pickles. Mom would can several jars of pickles every August or September when pickling cucumbers came ripe. She always sent us jars for Christmas. Sadly, I haven't picked up where Mom left off and we really miss Mom's pickles! Mom has offered to make them at Atria with the Chef and her fellow residents as a fun project.

Story submitted by Judy Snyder, pictured here with her mother, Atria Tamalpais Creek resident Edythe Halliday

Hot German Cole Slaw

Prep Time: 10 minutes | Cook Time: 30 minutes | Servings: 4

Ingredients:

1 egg
3 tbsp. vinegar
3 tbsp. sugar
3 tbsp. butter
½ head cabbage
salt and pepper to taste

Preparation:

Finely shred green cabbage and set aside.

Crack 1 egg into a small double boiler pan. Add vinegar, sugar and butter.

Whisk ingredients together, cooking over low-medium heat, constantly stirring until the mixture is very creamy and hot.

Pour this over the bed of cabbage and stir it up.

Let sit for at least 30 minutes before serving. Enjoy!

My grandmother's family was from Germany. She fixed a lot of sweet and sour salads. I remember standing on a footstool in front of her stove, learning how to make this slaw that was topped with a boiled, hot dressing. My job was to make sure that the mixture was constantly moving so that the egg would blend with the other ingredients. All during this process, my grandmother would talk to me. I still have fond memories of our cooking together.

Teresa Saltzman, Atria Daly City Executive Director

Mom's Scalloped Potatoes

Prep Time: 30 minutes | Cook Time: 1 hours | Servings: 6 – 8

Ingredients:

4 large potatoes, peeled and sliced

pinch of flour

salt and pepper to taste

1 stick butter

1 large onion, sliced

1 lb. cheddar cheese, shredded

milk

Preparation:

Place potatoes in bottom of 9"x 13" pan. Dust with flour. Sprinkle with salt and pepper.

Add dabs of butter, a layer of onions and shredded cheese. Repeat layers.

Add milk until you see it under the top layer of the potatoes. Make sure milk does not seep onto the top layer as this will make the dish soggy.

Cover with aluminum foil and bake at 350°F for 45 minutes. Remove aluminum foil and bake for an additional 15 minutes.

When I think of Mom, I always think of her scalloped potatoes. They are really good, especially the second time around. I miss my mom's cooking!

Story submitted by Mary Woodruff, daughter of Atria Johnson Ferry resident Carolyn Schlup, pictured here

Mushroom and Cranberry Stuffing

Prep Time: 20 minutes | Cook Time: 50 minutes | Servings: 8

Ingredients:

2 tbsp. olive oil, divided
1 large box fresh baby portobello mushrooms, quartered
1 ½ c. onions, chopped
1 tbsp. garlic, minced
¼ c. fresh parsley, chopped
2 tbsp. fresh sage, chopped
1 pkg. dried cranberries
1 bag herb-seasoned stuffing mix
1 can College Inn® chicken broth
¼ c. margarine, cut into pieces

Preparation:

Heat 1 tablespoon of oil. Add baby portobello mushrooms and cook for 5 minutes until lightly browned. Transfer mushrooms to a large mixing bowl. Heat remaining 1 tablespoon of oil and add onions and garlic. Sauté until onions are soft and lightly browned. Stir in parsley, sage and cranberries. Cook for another 2 minutes and transfer into bowl. Stir in stuffing mix, broth and margarine. Mix thoroughly.

Cover and refrigerate overnight.

The next day, remove from refrigerator and place mixture in greased 9"x 13" baking dish. Cover with foil and bake in oven at 350°F for 50 minutes.

I found this recipe back in 1990, when new family members would not partake of "the in-turkey stuffing." It became such a success that I continue to use it along with the normal bread sausage dressing.

The cooking club here at Atria Cranford made it in 2010. It was very successful, and many of the staff members asked for the recipe.

Lois Van Etten, Atria Cranford resident

Potato and Cheese Pierogi

Prep Time: 2 hours | Cook Time: 10 – 20 minutes | Servings: 8

Ingredients:

Dough:

3 c. all-purpose flour

1 c. water

1 tbsp. butter or oil

3 eggs, whole

Filling:

3 potatoes, peeled

1 large onion, diced

3 tbsp. butter, unsalted

3 tbsp. bakers cheese (substitute
    cream cheese)

1 tbsp. salt

1 tbsp. pepper

Preparation:

Dough: Combine flour, half the water, butter (or oil) and eggs in a large bowl. Stir vigorously to incorporate the eggs. Slowly stir in the remaining water until a dough ball begins to form. If the dough is too dry, add a little more water, a few drops at a time, until it comes together. Lift and stretch the dough until it becomes smooth and is somewhat sticky inside, about 3 minutes. Do not overwork. When the dough is ready, cover and set aside to prepare the filling.

Filling: Cook peeled potatoes in slightly salted water. Mash while hot and let chill. In a skillet, brown onion in butter. Then mix together potatoes, cheese, sautéed onion, salt and pepper.

Pierogi: Go back to the dough, forming into balls 1 ½" to 2" in diameter. Lightly flour the top of each dough ball. Roll out with a rolling pin into a 3" round, approximately ⅛" thick. Hold the dough in one hand and place a spoonful of filling into the center. Fold in half to enclose and pinch the edges securely together. Be sure there are no openings along the edges or the filling will boil out.

Boil a large pot of salted water while continuing to fill the remaining pierogi until all ingredients run out. Gently lower pierogi into rapidly boiling water 3 – 5 at a time and cook for a few minutes until they float to the surface. Remove with a slotted spoon and continue until all pierogi are prepared. Serve fresh with melted butter or sauté in butter until lightly browned.

Pierogi are traditional Polish dumplings most often filled with either sauerkraut or potato and cheese. I fondly remember my mother making potato and cheese pierogi for Friday night suppers. Following in my mother's footprints, I made pierogi for my family as well. I was born and raised in Chicago. My family attended St. Adalbert Polish Church. In preparation for the parish festivals, I would join 25 other women to make thousands of pierogi to sell at the feast. No matter how many we made, it was never enough. They all sold out on the first day of the feast!

Rose Czaplewski, Atria Aquidneck Place resident

Potato Pancakes

Prep Time: 30 minutes | Cook Time: 30 minutes | Servings: 6

Ingredients:

4 potatoes
1 onion
1 egg
1 tsp. salt
1 – 2 tbsp. flour

Preparation:

Grate potatoes and onion into a strainer. Drain and squeeze potatoes to get all the liquid out and place in bowl.

Mix in egg, salt and enough flour to make the mixture thick (depends on size of potatoes).

Heat oil in a skillet and drop potato mixture in mounds into the hot oil. Flatten to make pancakes.

Fry until golden brown and turn over. Fry other side to golden.

If you desire, salt the hot pancakes or serve unsalted with applesauce.

Everyone looked forward to my potato pancakes when I made them. Grating those potatoes on the old grater wasn't easy, and I often nicked my knuckles. One day, I decided I was going to make potato pancakes, but I didn't have any flour. I only needed one tablespoon. I called a neighbor and asked her to give me "mell," which is flour in Yiddish. I made the pancakes with what she gave me and they tasted awful! After all my hard work and the children's anticipation, we had nothing! I found out that she gave me "vell," not "mell" – she gave me a powder for cleaning dishes!

Sarah Katz, Atria Inn at Lakewood resident

Pretzel Strawberry Salad

rep Time: 45 – 60 minutes | Cook Time: 10 minutes | Servings: 12 – 15

ngredients:

2 ¼ c. thin pretzels, chopped

1 ½ c. walnuts, chopped

½ c. margarine

3 tbsp. brown sugar

8 oz. Cool Whip®

8 oz. cream cheese

½ c. sugar

2 c. water

6 oz. strawberry JELL-O®

16 oz. strawberries, frozen

Preparation:

Spray 9"x 13" pan with PAM® or grease with margarine. Put pretzels and walnuts on bottom of pan. Melt margarine and brown sugar together and pour over pretzels.

Bake at 350°F for 10 minutes. Let cool.

Mix together Cool Whip, cream cheese and sugar.

Spread over pretzels and refrigerate for 30 minutes.

Add JELL-O to 2 cups boiling water and dissolve. Add frozen strawberries. Pour JELL-O mixture over pretzels and chill overnight.

This is a staple of all Bauer family gatherings. My family has brought this to Atria Northgate Park several times for the residents here to try and everyone always wants more!

Irene Bauer, Atria Northgate Park resident

Rice Balls

Prep Time: 45 minutes | Cook Time: 30 minutes | Makes: 20

Ingredients:

1 stick butter

4 oz. tomato paste

2 c. water

1 c. white rice

salt and pepper to taste

3 eggs

¼ c. cheese, parmesan

1 small pkg. cheese, mozzarella (cut into small squares)

bread crumbs

parsley, dried

vegetable oil (or any frying oil)

Preparation:

Melt the butter in a saucepan, being careful not to let it brown. In another pan, heat tomato paste on medium to high, stirring until a little brown. Add the water to the tomato paste and bring to a boi Add the butter. Add the rice. Cook until water evaporates, stirring often so the rice doesn't stick. Salt and pepper to taste. Take the rice off the heat and add one of the eggs, stirring briskly. Stir in the parmesan cheese. Put the rice in a bowl and refrigerate overnight

The next day, prepare the bread crumbs with dried parsley and some more parmesan cheese in a bowl. Beat the other two eggs in a bowl. Remove the rice from the refrigerator and, with damp hands, take a little rice and place a piece of the mozzarella cheese in the center of the rice. Take more rice and cover the cheese and shape into a ball. Roll the ball in the bread crumbs and then the eggs and then the bread crumbs again.

Fry the rice balls in the oil until golden brown. They taste best whe eaten immediately, but can be reheated in the oven.

Rice balls are a family favorite and are served at all our holiday meals. When my grandchildren were younger, they would stand around and watch me fry these so they could have the first ones out of the frying pan. They are time-consuming to make, and now one of my granddaughters has taken up the task of providing them at all our family gatherings. These are so popular in our family that my granddaughter has to double the recipe at holidays.

Ann Rodolico, Atria Stamford resident

Rice Pilaf

Prep Time: 5 minutes | Cook Time: 40 – 45 minutes | Servings: 6

Ingredients:

1 stick butter, plus 1 tbsp., divided

2 vermicelli nests

1 c. long grain rice

2 c. chicken broth

salt and pepper, to taste

1/16 tsp. cumin

1/2 c. sliced almonds (optional)

Preparation:

In a sauté pan, melt a stick of butter. Sauté vermicelli nests in butter until brown, and break nests into smaller pieces with spoon.

Add long grain rice to vermicelli and sauté until brown.

In a separate skillet, boil chicken broth until bubbling hot. Add vermicelli and rice to the chicken broth, cover and simmer for 20 – 25 minutes.

Remove from heat and add a pinch (about 1/16 of a teaspoon) of salt, pepper and cumin. Finish by topping with 1 tablespoon of butter. For an extra treat, add almonds to the mix.

This dish is a flavor from my traditional Armenian background. I especially loved holidays, when family would come and my mother would cook traditional dishes such as shish kebab, boreg and the very delicious Armenian sweet bread, choreg.

My mother's wonderful rice pilaf is a favorite. When this was cooking in her pot, you could smell it for miles. My mother would pitch a fit if anyone dared open the cover of the rice before it was finished cooking, and she always stressed to wait until the broth was bubbling hot before adding it to the rice. "You have to *hear* it bubble," she would say.

Margaret Dunnett, Atria Longmeadow Place resident

Spicy Hot Black-Eyed Peas

Prep Time: 15 minutes | Cook Time: 30 minutes | Servings: 6

Ingredients:

- 1 lb. fresh or frozen shelled black-eyed peas
- ½ c. water
- 3 slices bacon
- 1 lb. canned tomatoes, un-drained and chopped
- 1 c. onion, chopped
- 1 large green pepper, chopped
- 1 clove garlic, crushed
- 1 tsp. salt
- 1 tsp. cumin, ground
- 1 tsp. dry mustard
- ½ tsp. curry powder
- ½ tsp. chili powder
- ½ tsp. black pepper
- parsley, for garnish

Preparation:

Combine peas and water in a pot. Bring to a boil. Cover and reduce heat to simmer for 10 minutes (or until almost tender). Drain and set aside.

Cook bacon in a large skillet until crisp. Remove bacon and crush.

In the same skillet, sauté onions, garlic and green peppers. Stir in peas and add all the spices. Bring to boil. Reduce heat to simmer for 20 minutes, stirring occasionally. Pour into serving dish. Sprinkle crumbled bacon and parsley over dish.

Our grown children, Winston and Lois, requested that I get my recipes together so they could prepare dishes they had eaten while growing up. My wish for you is that you enjoy serving your family interesting food and that you have a long and happy life.

Nell Holmes,
Atria Weston Place resident

Spoonbread

Prep Time: 10 minutes | Cook Time: 45 minutes | Servings: 10

Ingredients:

- 2 ½ c. water, boiling
- 1 c. cornmeal
- 2 tsp. salt
- 5 eggs
- 2 c. milk
- 1 stick butter

Preparation:

Pour boiling water over combined cornmeal and salt. Stir fast and mix well.

Beat eggs and milk together and add to meal mixture.

Melt stick of butter in 9"x 13" baking dish.

Pour half the melted butter into meal mixture and pour mixture into pan.

Bake at 350°F for 45 minutes.

Spoonbread will still appear a bit wet when it is done. Enjoy!

This is my wife's recipe and she always made it when she fried fish for our family. I believe she got this recipe from her mother. It signified "home" when we had fish for dinner. I have never had this particular dish anywhere else. It is a bit of a combination between cornbread and corn pudding. Enjoy!

Raymond Shaw, Atria San Pablo resident

Sweet Onion Pie

Prep Time: 10 – 15 minutes | Cook Time: 45 minutes | Servings: 6 – 8

Ingredients:

1 c. saltine cracker crumbs
5 tbsp. butter, melted
2 ½ c. onions, thinly sliced
2 tbsp. vegetable oil
2 eggs
¾ c. milk
salt and pepper to taste
¼ c. cheddar cheese, shredded

Preparation:

Combine crumbs and butter and press into 8" pan. Bake for 8 minutes at 350°F degrees.

Sauté onions in oil until soft and pour into shell.

Mix eggs, milk, and salt and pepper, and pour over onions. Top with cheese.

Bake at 350°F degrees for 45 minutes.

My mother-in-law used to make this dish for special occasions. My children grew up loving it and my husband looked forward to eating it!

Pat Joiner, Atria Richardson resident

Torta di Patate

Prep Time: 15 – 20 minutes | Cook Time: 40 minutes | Servings: 4 – 6

Ingredients:

2 lbs. potatoes

pinch of salt

pinch of flour

olive oil for frying

Preparation:

Peel and rinse potatoes, and then boil for about 20 minutes. Grate potatoes and add a pinch of salt. If dry, add a drop of water. Add pinch of flour. Mix well.

When frying, keep an eye on the temperature, as olive oil heats up faster than vegetable oil. Have enough oil in the pan to cover the torte and allow for even browning. Pan fry ¼ cup of flattened potato mixture at a time, cooking until golden brown.

Place on a plate covered with paper towels and pat to absorb excess oil.

The kitchen was an important part of my childhood. There, as a little girl in Revo, Italy, I would sit on the stone floor of my mother's kitchen. I eagerly watched her, learning northern Italian cooking and a culinary blend of Italy and Switzerland/Austria. We would make sauerkraut from scratch in large wooden barrels, whose insides were layered with cabbage and salt. We'd let the sauerkraut ferment for up to three months at a time.

At age 23, I moved to Brooklyn, New York, and brought my love of cooking with me. I would read every cookbook I could get my hands on and developed a continental flair in my meals with neighborhood girlfriends. My husband of 45 years and my family supported my culinary experiments, even though they didn't always turn out well. This Torta di Patate is one they did enjoy, and most weeks, I had to make it two or three times! It's a delicious food that can accompany other side dishes for a savory meal.

Catherine Rigatti, Atria Del Sol resident

Yumma's Potatoes

Prep Time: 45 minutes | Cook Time: 45 minutes | Servings: 10 – 12

Ingredients:

3 lbs. potatoes
2 c. mayonnaise
1 medium yellow onion, chopped
½ lb. bacon, cooked crisp
1 c. black or green olives, sliced
1 ½ c. cheddar cheese, shredded

Preparation:

Boil the potatoes for 15 – 20 minutes until cooked through. Let cool, then peel and slice into a bowl.

Mix with enough mayonnaise to moisten.

Add chopped onion to taste. Add any or all of the following to taste: crisp-cooked, crumbled bacon, sliced black or green olives.

Spoon into a greased casserole dish and cover with a generous layer of shredded cheddar cheese.

Bake at 350°F for 30 minutes or until heated through.

I made these potatoes for family events for years. When my grandchildren were old enough to ask for favorite foods, they would ask me to make this dish, and as they call me "Yumma," my dish became known as "Yumma's" potatoes.

Norma Love, Atria Marland Place resident

Baked Goods and Desserts

The bread that brings comfort to a neighbor during a difficult time. The candy that lifts the spirits of soldiers overseas. The cake that somehow disappears even when everyone claims they can't eat another bite.

A Cake to Build a Dream On

Prep Time: 15 minutes | Cook Time: 20 minutes | Servings: 16 – 20

Ingredients:

Cake Batter:

2 c. flour

2 c. sugar

2 sticks Crisco®

4 tbsp. cocoa

1 c. water

½ c. buttermilk

2 eggs, slightly beaten

1 tsp. vanilla

1 tsp. baking soda

Icing:

1 stick Crisco

⅓ c. milk

1 box powdered sugar

¼ tsp. vanilla

¼ c. cocoa

Preparation:

Preheat oven to 400°F. Place flour and sugar in a bowl, then set aside. Mix together and bring to a boil, Crisco, cocoa and water. Pour over flour mixture. Add buttermilk, eggs, vanilla and baking soda. Mix all ingredients until smooth. Pour into 9" x 13" pan. Bake for 20 minutes.

Icing: Mix Crisco and milk. Bring to a boil. Add powdered sugar, vanilla and cocoa. Beat well. Spread over cake when icing has cooled.

I grew up on a farm in rural Greenfield, Oklahoma. Though we did not have much, it was a home built on love. Here is the story of how my mother captured the heart of my father with this chocolate cake recipe!

Daddy and mother met at a box social sometime before World War I. A box social was a fundraiser in which the young ladies would decorate a small box with ribbons, lace, crepe paper, buttons and flowers, then fill the box with something they had made, to catch the eye of the fellows. The gentlemen would bid on the boxes; the highest bidder would win the box and its contents. The young lady who brought the box would then reveal her identity and together they enjoyed what she had fixed. Daddy bought mother's box (with the chocolate cake inside)! They were married two years later when he returned from the frontlines of World War I. A lifetime of wonderful memories was started with a bite of this decadent cake; I hope you enjoy it as much as I do.

Betty Tillman, Atria Summit Ridge resident, pictured here with her daughter Donna and granddaughter Jessee

Alma's Coffee Cake

Prep Time: 20 minutes | Cook Time: 20 – 30 minutes | Servings: 10

Ingredients:

Cake Batter:
1 c. sugar
3 tbsp. butter, melted
¼ tsp. salt
1 egg
1 c. milk
2 c. flour, sifted
1 tbsp. baking powder
Topping:
¼ c. white sugar
2 tbsp. butter, softened
2 tbsp. flour
2 tsp. cinnamon

Preparation:

Stir 1 cup of sugar with 3 tablespoons of melted butter. Add ¼ tablespoon of salt then stir. Add 1 egg to milk then stir.

Pour in egg and milk mixture then stir. Add sifted flour and stir. Add baking powder then stir.

Pour into baking pan. Spread 2 tablespoons of butter over batter.

Sprinkle white sugar, flour and cinnamon over batter.

Bake at 375°F for 20 – 30 minutes. Cut into squares and serve.

My mother's coffee cake was my first attempt at baking. Yes, I remember helping my mother in the kitchen, but baking? I still remember that bright, warm kitchen and the big, yellow fiesta mixing bowl (there were no mixers when I was seven years old); turning the sifter handle with the flour and baking powder falling gently; stirring the batter until my arm was tired; and all the while mother sitting at the kitchen table, smiling and telling me how. Then, finally, from the oven came the most delicious smell and with a toothpick, we decided it was done. Nothing ever tasted as good as we sat around the breakfast table those Sunday mornings so long ago!

Ruth Suttner, Atria Woodbridge resident

Anadama Bread

Prep Time: 1 ½ hours | Cook Time: 45 – 55 minutes | Servings: 1 loaf

ngredients:

1 c. milk, warm
½ c. water, warm
½ c. cornmeal
5 tbsp. molasses
3 tbsp. butter, melted
3 ½ c. flour
1 pkg. rapid rise yeast (also called instant yeast)
2 tsp. salt

Preparation:

Bring milk and water to a boil in small saucepan. Slowly whisk in cornmeal.

Cook about 1 minute, stirring constantly, until mixture thickens. Transfer to a bowl and cool until just warm enough to touch, and then stir in molasses and butter.

Combine flour, yeast and salt in a bowl. Add cornmeal mixture and mix until it comes together. Knead for about 8 – 10 minutes with a mixer that has a dough hook, or by hand, until dough is smooth and elastic.

Place dough in an oiled bowl and cover with a plastic wrap. Let rise for about 1 ½ hours, until doubled. Shape into a loaf and place in a greased 9"x 5" loaf pan. Cover with plastic wrap sprayed with PAM® and let rise until doubled.

Bake in an oven preheated to 350°F on the lower third rack. Bake for 45 – 55 minutes or until golden brown.

Cool loaf in pan on a rack for 15 minutes. Then, turn out onto rack and cool to room temperature.

Anadama is a New England bread made with molasses and cornmeal, and is delicious as is or toasted. The turkey sandwiches the day after Thanksgiving were almost as special as the main event. My mom, who was a wonderful baker, would always make a couple of loaves of anadama bread for my dad to have the next day for lunch.

Story submitted by Marie Piraino, daughter of Atria Marina Place resident Jim Piraino, pictured here

Anginette Cookies

Prep Time: 20 minutes | Cook Time: 12 – 15 minutes | Servings: 24

Ingredients:

Dough:
½ c. spry (shortening)
¾ c. sugar
3 large eggs
pinch of salt
1 tsp. lemon or vanilla flavoring
½ c. orange juice
3 tsp. baking powder
¼ tsp. baking soda
3 c. flour (plus 1 c. flour for adding until not sticky)
Glaze:
1 c. confectioners' sugar
1 tbsp. orange juice

Preparation:

Mix spry, sugar, eggs, salt, lemon or vanilla flavoring and orange juice with electric mixer until well blended.

Then, using a spoon, add baking powder, baking soda and flour. Add extra flour until dough is no longer sticky.

Spoon dough by teaspoonfuls onto ungreased baking sheet.

Bake for 12 – 15 minutes at 350°F.

Mix glaze ingredients to a smooth consistency. When cookies are cool, frost with glaze.

This recipe for Anginette cookies has been in the family for years and years. When my mother cooked, she was not able to measure things as she was blind. I needed to watch her make the cookies to figure out the measurements. I still say that you need to add more flour until it feels "right," but who besides me knows what that is? We have made these cookies for every bake sale and fundraiser here at Atria Larson Place for the past few years.

Ann Massaro, Atria Larson Place resident

Anise Christmas Cookies

Prep Time: 1 ½ hours | Cook Time: 8 – 10 minutes | Servings: 24

Ingredients:

2 eggs
½ c. butter
1 c. sugar
½ tsp. salt
2 ½ c. flour
2 – 3 tbsp. milk
few drops of anise oil

Preparation:

Beat eggs, add butter and sugar, then thoroughly mix with salt and flour.

Chill for at least an hour in a sealable bag or plastic wrap.

Preheat oven to 375°F.

Flour a flat rolling surface, roll out dough to approximately ¼" thickness and cut out cookies.

Bake on baking sheet for 8 – 10 minutes. Allow cookies to cool. Frost if desired.

This unique cut-out Christmas cookie has been a traditional yuletide treat in my husband's family since the 1800s. Today, the tradition is carried on by our children. Anise oil (or extract) contributes to the uniqueness of this buttery cookie, which is delicious with icing.

Gigi Mauter, Atria San Juan Engage Life Director

Anzac Biscuits

Prep Time: 20 minutes | Cook Time: 15 – 20 minutes | Servings: 15

Ingredients:

1 c. flour
½ c. sugar
1 c. rolled oats, not instant
½ tsp. baking soda
½ c. chopped walnuts
¾ c. coconut
2 tbsp. honey or golden syrup
½ c. butter
2 tbsp. boiling water

Preparation:

Mix together flour, sugar, oats, baking soda, walnuts and coconut.

Melt butter and honey. Make a well in the center of the flour mixture and stir in liquids.

Spoon dough by tablespoonfuls onto two greased baking sheets.

Bake 15 – 20 minutes at 350°F.

During World War I, a few women in New Zealand and Australia got together to decide just what treat they could create to cheer up their loved ones overseas. The result was a cookie called "Anzac Biscuits" (short for: Australia and New Zealand Army Corps). This was the treat of all treats. Anzac biscuits were shipped well into World War II and were the most often requested. They are a crunchy, nutty, delightful biscuit. The biscuits traveled well; I made them for my husband and he always looked forward to a care package to share with the men in his barracks.

Gloria Walton, Atria Covell Gardens resident

Apple Betty

Prep Time: 20 minutes | Cook Time: 45 minutes | Servings: 6

Ingredients:

4 c. sliced apples (Cortland or McIntosh preferred)

¼ c. orange juice

1 c. sugar

¾ c. all-purpose flour

½ tsp. cinnamon

½ tsp. nutmeg

½ c. butter

Preparation:

Mound apples in a buttered 9" pie plate.

Sprinkle with the orange juice.

To make the topping, combine sugar, flour, cinnamon and nutmeg.

Cut in the butter until the mixture is crumbled and spread evenly over the apples.

Bake in oven at 375°F for 45 minutes or until golden brown.

This was my husband's favorite recipe, so I made it often. Apples were very plentiful in New Hampshire, especially in the fall, and I used them often. I remember when my daughter was about three years old, I had two half-bushel bags of apples sitting on the floor in the kitchen. When I went to get some out of the bag, I found she had taken bites out of about five apples in each bag! I have so many fond memories of baking with my daughter – we made apple betty, pies, applesauce, apple brownies…

Linda Stuart, Atria MerryWood resident

Auntie Cake

Prep Time: 20 minutes | Cook Time: 35 minutes | Servings: 18 – 20

Ingredients:

Cake:

⅓ c. cocoa

½ c. hot water

½ c. vegetable oil

1 tsp. vanilla

¼ tsp. almond extract

1 ½ c. buttermilk

2 tsp. soda in 1 tbsp. water

2 c. flour

1 ½ c. sugar

¼ tsp. salt

Icing:

3 tbsp. cocoa

1 c. sugar

⅓ c. milk

1 tbsp. butter

1 c. powdered sugar

1 tsp. vanilla

¼ tsp. almond extract

½ c. pecans, chopped

Preparation:

Dissolve ⅓ cup of cocoa in ½ cup of hot water. Add in all other liquids. Let it cool. Sift flour, sugar and salt 6 times.

Place dry mixture in a mixing bowl. Lightly blend all ingredients in mixing bowl. Add to greased cake pan (9"x 13") or cupcake pans and bake at 325°F for 35 minutes. This recipe originated at sea level (may need to cook at 350°F).

While the cake is cooling, prepare the icing. Mix cocoa and sugar. Add milk and butter and bring to a boil. Boil 3 minutes, then remove from heat. Add powdered sugar, vanilla, almond extract and pecans. Stir well.

Frost cake or cupcakes while still warm. Let cool before slicing.

My mother's aunt used to prepare this cake for family dinners or parties. Then my mother took up the tradition. At one time, Mother had the recipe memorized because she made it so often. It is easy to prepare and loved by everyone in our family. It is simple to make and is a great chocolate cake.

Kay Cargile,
Atria Vista del Rio resident

Baklava

Prep Time: 20 minutes | Cook Time: 50 minutes | Servings: 16

Ingredients:

Pastry:

1 (16 oz.) pkg. phyllo dough

1 c. butter

1 c. nuts, chopped (walnuts, cashews or pistachios)

¼ tsp. allspice

¼ tsp. cinnamon

⅛ tsp. cloves, ground

⅛ tsp. nutmeg

Glaze:

1 c. water

1 c. sugar

½ c. honey

Preparation:

Heat oven to 350°F. Toss nuts and spices together. Place 2 sheets of phyllo dough on greased baking sheet. Butter thoroughly and layer another sheet of phyllo on top of buttered sheets, repeating 8 times. Sprinkle half the nut mixture on top of phyllo. Cover nut mixture with 2 layers of buttered phyllo dough. Repeat and sprinkle rest of nut mixture over phyllo. Cover nut mixture with remaining phyllo dough, buttering between each sheet. Cut baklava into squares or triangles.

Bake 50 minutes. While baklava is baking, make glaze by boiling water and sugar until dissolved. Add honey and simmer for 20 minutes. Remove baklava from oven and cover with glaze.

My dad was a self-taught pastry chef who specialized in Middle Eastern desserts. I remember growing up and having baklava, a staple in our home. This was my dad's specialty and, I think, one of his favorites to eat. He baked it for all special occasions and catered from home after he retired. It was common to see 15 baking sheets of baklava (among other desserts) in the kitchen on a weekend my dad was catering. My father passed away in 2000, and unfortunately, he never wrote down his recipes. My older siblings and I tried to replicate this recipe and I think we came very close. I have tried other baklava recipes, but none measure up to this. This recipe takes me back to a simple time and back to my parents' kitchen: preteen and without a care in the world.

Story submitted by, Zeinab Donner, Atria Sunnyvale Executive Director and daughter of Salim Elachkar, pictured here

Banana Nut Bread

Prep Time: 20 minutes | Cook Time: 1 hour | Servings: 1 loaf

Ingredients:

½ c. vegetable oil
1 c. sugar
2 eggs, beaten
3 ripe bananas
3 tbsp. milk
½ tsp. vanilla extract
2 c. all-purpose flour
1 tsp. baking soda
½ tsp. baking powder
½ tsp. salt
½ c. walnuts, chopped

Preparation:

Preheat oven to 350°F. Grease and flour a 9"x 5" loaf pan. In a large bowl, beat oil and sugar together. Add eggs, one at a time, beating well (15 seconds each).

In separate bowl, add and mix well bananas, milk and vanilla. Mix well in a third bowl all dry ingredients, or sift together, flour, baking soda, baking powder and salt. Alternate adding banana mix and dry mix to large bowl (mix for 2 minutes). Add chopped walnuts; stir well (15 seconds). Pour batter into prepared pan.

Bake for about 60 minutes or until toothpick inserted in center comes out clean. Cool loaf 8 – 10 minutes. Remove loaf from pan. Place on wire rack to cool completely. Store overnight before cutting.

Note: ½ teaspoon lemon extract or 2 teaspoons lemon juice may also be added. This is the way my dad would make it. If a drier loaf is desired, turn oven off after baking, leave oven door open, and let loaf stay in oven to cool for 8 – 10 minutes.

I love to bake cookies and cakes for my family! I really enjoy experimenting with different ingredients and giving each recipe my own special twist. Banana Nut Bread is one of my favorites. I hope you enjoy it!

Joseph Zimbalatti, Atria Glen Cove resident

Blueberry Biscuits

Prep Time: 20 minutes | Cook Time: 12 – 15 minutes | Servings: 14 – 16

Ingredients:

2 c. flour
3 tsp. baking powder
1 tsp. salt
4 tbsp. shortening
1 c. blueberries
¾ c. milk

Preparation:

Sift and measure flour. Add baking powder and salt then sift again.

Cut in shortening until dry ingredients resemble coarse cornmeal. Add blueberries, stirring gently with a fork. Add enough milk to make dough soft and until all flour is blended in.

Turn out onto board and knead lightly for about 30 seconds. Turn smooth side up and pat dough or roll to ½" thickness. Cut with floured round cutter.

Transfer cut-outs to greased baking sheet. Place 1" apart for crusty delicious biscuits, or barely touching for softer biscuits with less crust.

Bake at 450°F for 12 – 15 minutes. Butter tops of the baked biscuits and serve at once.

Blueberry biscuits were a breakfast favorite at our family farm. They are best made with Maine's incomparable, tiny wild blueberries picked just before the biscuits are made. I would pass out the same enameled tin cups my mother and aunt had used to pick berries when they were children, and send the breakfast crowd out to get enough berries for the biscuits, snacks and perhaps a pie. I would heat the oven, assemble the ingredients and set the table while they were picking, and be able to take the biscuits right out of the oven shortly after everyone sat down. No matter how many blueberry biscuits I made, there were never any left.

Ruth Hill, Atria Kennebunk resident

Blueberry Pie

Prep Time: 30 – 45 minutes | Cook Time: 35 – 45 minutes | Servings: 8 –

Ingredients:

Crust:
1 c. all-purpose flour
½ tsp. salt
½ c. and 1 tbsp. shortening
2 – 3 tbsp. cold water
Pie Filling:
1 c. sugar
¼ c. all-purpose flour
½ tsp. cinnamon
3 c. blueberries, fresh
1 tsp. lemon juice
1 tbsp. butter or margarine

Preparation:

Heat oven to 425°F. Prepare pastry dough first and then filling.

Crust: Measure flour and salt into bowl; cut in shortening thoroughly. Sprinkle in water, 1 tablespoon at a time, mixing until all flour is moistened and dough almost cleans side of bowl. Separate and roll on a floured surface.

Filling: Stir together sugar, flour and cinnamon. Mix in blueberries. Turn into pastry-lined pie pan; sprinkle with lemon juice and dot with butter. Cover with top crust, which has slits in it; seal and flute edges. (You can cover edges with foil to prevent browning. If foil is used, remove for last 15 minutes of cooking time.) Bake 35 – 45 minutes. Cool and enjoy!

My mother used to take my brothers, my sister and me blueberry picking out in Farmington, Michigan. Mom would pay us five cents a quart to pick the berries. At that time, five cents bought five pieces of Bazooka® bubble gum, a large candy bar and other sweet goodies. Mom would make pies, muffins or use the blueberries at breakfast on the side.

It wasn't until I was much older that I realized how much work went into picking a quart of berries! When I was older, Mom would have me make dozens of pies to freeze throughout the summer: rhubarb, blueberry, cherry (we had our own trees) and peach. To this day, I continue to enjoy baking pies!

Story submitted by Pat McKinley, daughter of Atria Cutter Mill resident Nora Hainline, pictured here

Blueberry Summer Pie

Prep Time: 30 minutes | Cook Time: 45 minutes | Servings: 8

Ingredients:

1 pie shell, baked
⅔ c. sugar
¼ tsp. salt
2 tbsp. cornstarch
⅔ c. boiling water
2 c. blueberries
2 tbsp. butter
1 tbsp. lemon juice
1 c. whipping cream
2 – 4 tbsp. confectioners' sugar, to taste
1 – 2 tsp. vanilla, to taste

Preparation:

Make your own pie shell or use store-bought pie shell; bake and set aside.

Filling, Part One:
Mix sugar, salt and cornstarch in sauce pan. Pour boiling water over the mixture. Add 1 cup of blueberries. Boil until thick and clear, stirring constantly. Add butter and lemon juice. Cool mixture completely. Add second cup of blueberries to cooled mixture. Set aside.

Filling, Part Two:
In a chilled bowl, whip cream until stiff, adding confectioners' sugar and vanilla. Place in pie shell, making a "nest" for the blueberry mixture.

Place the blueberry mixture on the whipped cream in the pie shell, leaving a rim of whipped cream around the perimeter. Chill pie several hours in refrigerator before serving.

Mom made blueberry summer pie as a special treat for family or guests. This cool and delicious dessert was very welcome on hot summer evenings.

Story submitted by Lisa Kleitz, daughter of Atria Riverdale resident Elsie Klitz, pictured here

Bubbe's Cookies (Mandelbread)

Prep Time: 15 minutes | Cook Time: 25 minutes | Servings: 36

Ingredients:

3 large eggs, separated
1 c. sugar
1 tsp. vanilla
1 c. vegetable oil
3 c. flour
3 tsp. baking powder
pinch of salt
1 c. almonds, crushed
¼ c. sugar and 1 tsp. cinnamon mixture

Preparation:

Preheat oven to 350°F.

Beat egg yolks well. Add sugar and mix. Add oil and vanilla. Stir to combine.

Beat egg whites until stiff and fold into egg yolk mixture. Sift flour with baking powder and salt, and add a little at a time, stirring to combine. Add and mix in crushed almonds.

Shape into 2 loaves and place on greased baking sheet. Sprinkle sugar-cinnamon mixture on top.

Bake 25 minutes at 350°F.

Slice into 1" pieces and put back in oven on a cookie sheet to toast both sides.

That familiar *cla-clunk, cla-clunk* of Bubbe and Grandpa's well-loved Dodge Dart® coming up the driveway meant one thing: the Bubbe cookies had arrived. There was a very specific routine to their arrival, a three-step process: Bubbe and Grandpa parked the car, waited for us to come outside to greet them, and then placed the Bubbe cookies into our eager, outstretched hands. They were freshly made in her apartment in the Bronx, and then safely packed for travel in empty strawberry containers lined with paper towels. The cookies crisped, crumbled and melted in our mouths!

Story submitted by Jacqueline & Sylvie Rosokoff, granddaughters of Atria Hamilton Heights resident Jean Schonfeld, pictured here

Bumbleberry Pie

Prep Time: 10 minutes | Cook Time: 45 minutes | Servings: 8

Ingredients:

- 2 (9") unbaked pie crusts
- 1 ⅓ c. white sugar
- ⅓ c. all-purpose flour
- 2 c. thinly sliced apples
- 1 c. fresh raspberries
- 1 c. fresh blackberries
- 1 c. fresh rhubarb, cut into 1" pieces

Preparation:

Preheat oven to 350°F.

Stir sugar and flour together in large bowl. Add apples, raspberries, blackberries and rhubarb.

Place first pie crust into bottom of pie pan.

Pour fruit mixture into pie crust. Cut the second pie crust into strips and cover the pie filling in lattice form. Trim excess and seal edges.

Bake at 350°F for about 45 minutes until crust is brown and apples are tender.

While on vacation, my wife and I stopped in Freeport, Maine. We had dinner in a quaint little restaurant. Bumbleberry pie was on the menu for dessert. We liked it so much we just had to have the recipe! We found a small book store which had an obscure cookbook; sure enough the recipe was there! Over the years, we have enjoyed making bumbleberry pie and reminiscing about our vacation.

Bob Clark, Atria Huntington resident

Burnt Sugar Cake with Caramel Frosting

Prep Time: 1 hour | Cook Time: 45 minutes | Servings: 12

Ingredients:

Burnt Sugar:	
1 c. sugar	
½ c. boiling water	
¾ c. cold water	
Cake:	
½ c. soft shortening	
1 ⅓ c. sugar	
3 large eggs	
2 ½ c. all-purpose flour, sifted	
2 ½ tsp. baking powder	
1 tsp. salt	
Caramel Frosting:	
6 tbsp. butter	
½ c. cream	
3 c. confectioners' sugar, sifted	
⅓ tsp. salt	
1 tsp. vanilla	

Preparation:

Prepare the burnt sugar: Place the sugar in a heavy pan. Cook over low heat, stirring constantly until the sugar melts and turns into a golden brown syrup. Remove from heat. Stir in the hot water. Be careful: the sugar mixture will be very hot. Set aside.

Prepare the cake: Take ¼ cup cooled burnt sugar mixture and add ¾ cup cold water to make 1 cup of the mixture. Set aside. Cream together shortening and sugar until fluffy. Add the 3 eggs and beat thoroughly. Sift together the flour, baking powder and salt. Add alternately to the creamed mixture with the rest of the burnt sugar mixture. Pour into a prepared pan (greased and floured). Bake at 350°F for 30 to 35 minutes in two 9" pans, or 35 to 45 minutes in a 9"x 13" pan.

Prepare caramel frosting: Heat together the butter and all of the remaining caramel mixture along with enough cream to equal ½ cup. Add sifted confectioners' sugar, salt and vanilla. Beat until smooth. Frost and enjoy!

When my sister, brother and I would come home from school when Mom had an off day from the hospital where she worked, we would sometimes be greeted by the delicious smell of burnt sugar syrup floating out from the kitchen. We knew that would mean a delicious dinner, and then a slice of wonderful burnt sugar cake with candy-like caramel frosting. What a sweet memory!

Story submitted by Judy Lanning, pictured here with her mother Atria Richardson resident Marion Lanning, and her siblings Carolyn and Earl

Caramel Popcorn Balls

Time: 45 minutes | Makes: 16

Ingredients:

- 4 qt. popped popcorn, unbuttered and unsalted
- ½ c. butter, melted
- 1 lb. light brown sugar
- ¾ c. Karo® syrup
- 2 c. small marshmallows
- 1 tsp. vanilla

Preparation:

On low heat, cook the butter, brown sugar and Karo syrup until it reaches the soft-ball stage – about 235°F on a candy thermometer. At this temperature, a little sugar syrup dropped into a glass of cold water will form a soft, flexible ball.

Remove from heat and add marshmallows and vanilla. Stir until marshmallows have melted.

When mixture has cooled to where it is safe to touch, but still warm, pour over popcorn in a large mixing bowl. Coat popcorn thoroughly.

Dip your hands in cool water so the caramel doesn't stick to you, and then form balls with the coated popcorn.

When I was young, Mom would cook up the caramel sauce while the kids popped the corn. Mom would pour the caramel over the popcorn and my dad had the job of making sure the popcorn was coated completely. My sisters and I would then dip our hands in cool water so the caramel wouldn't stick to us and we formed the balls. We did this every December and as we got older, we learned how to make the caramel and coat the popcorn. I make these popcorn balls every year with my husband and sons. My whole family comes to our house to carry on the tradition together. These popcorn balls are better than anything you'll find in the store.

Gina Lardie, Atria El Camino Gardens Engage Life Program Instructor

Carrot Cake with Cream Cheese Frosting

Prep Time: 30 minutes | Cook Time: 45 minutes | Servings: 8 – 12

Ingredients:

Cake:

1 ½ c. vegetable oil

2 c. sugar

4 eggs

2 c. flour

2 tsp. baking soda

1 tsp. salt

3 tsp. cinnamon

2 tsp. vanilla

3 c. carrots, grated

Frosting:

1 stick butter

8 oz. cream cheese

1 lb. confectioners' sugar

2 tsp. vanilla

Preparation:

Cake: Mix together all ingredients. Bake in three greased 8" layer pans for 45 minutes. Cool completely before frosting.

Frosting: Combine cream cheese and butter in food processor. Add vanilla. When thoroughly mixed, add sugar in gradually, and blend until smooth.

Assemble cake by spreading frosting between cake layers and over top and sides.

What a time that was! My husband had returned from World War II service and we still lived with my parents, although we did have our own room and bath. I had recently had a baby girl and of course, she needed my attention. One morning when it was raining outside I wanted to do something grand in the kitchen. I went through my mom's recipes and picked this dessert out.

Gladys Goldberg, Atria Cutter Mill resident

Chinese New Year Candy

Prep Time: 15 minutes | Cook Time: 10 minutes | Servings: 10 – 15

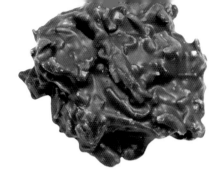

Ingredients:

- 1 (12 oz.) pkg. Nestle® toll house morsels
- 1 (11 oz.) pkg. Nestle butterscotch morsels
- 1 c. chow mein noodles
- 1 c. Spanish peanuts

Preparation:

Melt chocolate and butterscotch morsels in a double boiler.

Add noodles and peanuts, stirring constantly.

When coated, drop by tablespoonfuls onto waxed-paper-covered cookie sheet.

Refrigerate until hard.

When we lived in Hanover, Pennsylvania, I bought a cookbook through our church and this recipe was in it. We made it every Christmas and even now, 52 years later, it isn't Christmas for my family without this candy. Enjoy while waiting patiently for Santa!

Betty McGregor, Atria Windsor Woods resident

Christmas Pastry

Prep Time: 25 minutes | Cook Time: 1 hour | Servings: 6

Ingredients:

Crust Base:
½ c. butter, softened
1 c. all-purpose flour
2 tbsp. water

Topping:
½ c. butter
1 c. water
¼ c. sugar
1 tsp. almond flavoring
1 c. all-purpose flour
3 eggs

Glaze:
1 ½ c. powdered sugar
2 tbsp. water, peach schnapps, or vanilla extract

Preparation:

Crust Base: Preheat the oven to 350°F. Mix together the butter and flour until the mixture is in pea-sized crumbles. Sprinkle in water and gather into a ball. Split ball into 2 halves. Form each half into a rectangle. Place rectangles on a 12"x 16" cookie sheet, 3" apart. Pat these down to form a crust base.

Topping: Heat the butter and water into a rolling boil, then reduce heat to low. Stir in the sugar, flavoring and flour until the mixture forms a ball. Remove from heat and add in the eggs. Beat this mixture with a spatula until it is smooth and glossy. Spread half of this mixture on each rectangle crust. (Applying some fresh nutmeg, raw sugar or almonds to the crust before adding the topping can be tasty, too.) Bake the two rectangles with the topping for 1 hour at 350°F until crisp and brown. Periodically test doneness by inserting a knife into the crust.

Glaze (optional): Apply after removing pastry from oven. Mix together 1 ½ cups of powdered sugar and 2 tablespoons of water, peach schnapps or vanilla extract. Spread over pastries.

My Great-Aunt Sarah Elizabeth shared this recipe with my Dad who has made it every Christmas morning for as long as I can remember. We enjoy it with a dish of fresh ambrosia while opening our stockings from Santa.

Ronda Watson,
Atria Senior Living Vice President of Culinary Services

Coconut Cake

Prep Time: 30 – 45 minutes | Cook Time: 25 minutes | Servings: 12

Ingredients:

Cake:

1 c. butter

2 c. sugar

3 egg whites

2 whole eggs

3 c. flour

3 tsp. baking powder

¼ tsp. salt

1 ¼ c. coconut milk

Icing:

3 c. sugar

1 c. boiling water

1 ¼ c. coconut, finely grated

¼ c. coconut milk

1 tsp. vanilla extract

Preparation:

Cake: Cream butter and sugar until fluffy. Add eggs one at a time and blend together. In separate bowl, mix flour, baking powder and salt together. Then, alternate adding flour mixture and coconut milk to the first mixture. Pour evenly into three greased and floured 9" round cake pans and bake at 350°F for 18 – 20 minutes. Remove and cool.

Icing: Add sugar to boiling water and cook for 7 minutes, or until a thick syrup forms and coats spoon and forms a thread. Remove from heat. Add finely grated coconut, coconut milk and vanilla. Blend and set aside to cool.

Place first layer of cake on plate and, using a knife, make slits over entire cake and pour ⅛ cup coconut milk over first layer. Spoon small amounts of cooked coconut mixture over layer, then repeat process with second and third layer. Cover entire cake with remaining cooked mixture and sprinkle fresh coconut over entire cake.

My family used fresh coconut and ground the coconut themselves, and the cake was made one week prior to Christmas Day so the coconut flavor soaked into the cake. The recipe was passed down from generation to generation, starting sometime in the 1800s. After baking, the cake was put into a box and the box was then wrapped in a clean flour sack. The cake was stored under the bed because it was the coolest room in our home. Having a coconut cake for Christmas was a special treat and the anticipation created by the wait made it all that more delicious on Christmas Day. The smell throughout the house was heavenly.

Macie Barnes, Atria Willow Glen resident

Crepes Suzette

Prep Time: 1 hour | Cook Time: 1 hour | Servings: 20

Ingredients:

Crepes:

2 c. flour

1 c. seltzer water

2 egg yolks, beaten

Filling:

2 lbs. farmer's cheese, mashed

2 egg yolks, beaten

½ c. sugar, more or less to taste

zest of 1 lemon, or to taste

2 tsp. vanilla extract

Topping:

16 oz. sour cream

½ c. sugar

1 tsp. vanilla

zest of 1 lemon, or to taste

1 c. walnuts, finely chopped

Preparation:

To make the crepes, mix the flour, water and egg yolk together. Cover the bottom of a small Teflon® frying pan with the batter. Don't make crepes too thin. Cook until bubbly and slightly golden. Remove and stack on a plate and set aside. Continue to make the rest of the crepes, one at a time, stacking them on the plate.

To make the filling, blend the filling ingredients well in a mixing bowl. Spoon cheese mixture into crepes and roll up. Line crepes up in greased baking pan. Mix the topping ingredients together and cover the crepes with sour cream mixture. Top with a good amount of very finely chopped walnuts.

Bake at 325°F until it bubbles and sour cream mixture starts to brown (1 hour, more or less, depending on how chilled the sour cream is). This recipe can be made ahead of an event and refrigerated before cooking.

I was born in Hungary in 1924 and came to the United States with my husband in 1950. My recipe for crepes suzette was a big favorite of my sons and my husband; so much so, that they ate it out of the pan as I was taking it out of the oven! My husband was known for bringing guests home, and when I made the crepes, I had to remind him that he needed to "share." This is a recipe that I know by heart.

Ilona Rozsa, Atria Stamford resident

Crock-Pot Candy

Prep Time: 15 minutes | Cook Time: 2 ½ hours | Servings: 24 – 36

Ingredients:

16 oz. white almond bark
16 oz. chocolate almond bark
1 (12 oz.) pkg. chocolate chips
4 oz. Baker's German's Sweet Chocolate Bar®
12 – 15 oz. salted peanuts, dry roasted
12 – 15 oz. unsalted peanuts, dry roasted

Preparation:

Put all ingredients in Crock-Pot® but do not stir. Cover with lid. Cook on low temperature for 2 ½ hours.

Stir carefully and drop by the tablespoonful onto wax paper.

Cool completely. You can leave it sit on the wax paper overnight or wait about 2 hours to dry.

Gently remove pieces from wax paper and put in a cool place in airtight container.

A good friend of mine gave me this recipe. I thought she must be nuts to think you could just keep piling one ingredient on top of another, never stirring. You could look through the glass lid and it always looked like the first time you put the ingredients in: nothing had changed. Well, after 2 ½ hours cooking time, lift off the lid and it was ready to spoon out on the wax paper. It's a great piece of candy. Serve it with plenty of small plates and napkins.

June G. Schebler, Atria Hearthstone resident

Cuban Flan

Prep Time: 5 minutes | Cook Time: 45 minutes | Servings: 8

Ingredients:

6 eggs
12 oz. can evaporated milk
14 oz. can sweetened condensed milk
couple of drops of whole milk
couple of drops of vanilla
1 c. sugar

Preparation:

In blender, blend together eggs, evaporated milk, sweetened condensed milk, whole milk and vanilla.

Caramelize sugar in saucepan on low heat, then glaze a Bundt® cake pan with the caramel. Pour the flan mixture into the Bundt pan. Put the Bundt pan in another flat pan filled with hot water, as if you're making custard.

Bake in an oven at 350°F for 45 minutes. Let cool in a refrigerator for at least 2 hours.

Remove from refrigerator and flip the flan onto a serving plate.

I was living at Puerto Rico in the early 1970s. A family of Cuban refugees moved into a house next to mine. Their youngest son, who was 15, was in a motorcycle accident and was injured very badly. I wanted to let them know I was concerned and show my support, but I couldn't speak Spanish and they didn't know English. I decided to bake a cake and give it to them. Some time later, the boy's mother brought us the flan to show her appreciation. I asked for the recipe and, as you can imagine, it took us almost the whole day to write it down because of the language barrier. Ever since, this dessert has been a favorite dish in our family.

Heather Evans, Atria Sunlake resident

Estonia Easter Bread

Prep Time: 30 minutes, plus rising time | Cook Time: 30 – 35 minutes
Servings: 12

Ingredients:

2 ¼ – 3 ¼ cups unsifted flour, divided
¼ c. sugar
1 tsp. salt
1 pkg. active dry yeast
⅔ c. milk
2 tbsp. butter
7 eggs
¼ c. melted butter
food coloring

Preparation:

Dye 5 eggs (still raw) in Easter colors using food coloring. Set aside.

In a large bowl, thoroughly mix 1 cup flour, sugar, salt and dry yeast. Combine milk and butter in a saucepan and cook over low heat until warm. Gradually add to dry ingredients and beat 2 minutes at a medium speed, occasionally scraping down the bowl. Add 2 eggs and ½ cup flour (or enough flour to make a thick batter). Beat at high speed for 2 minutes, scraping bowl occasionally. Stir in enough flour to make a soft dough.

Turn out onto lightly floured board, kneading until smooth and elastic, about 8 – 10 minutes. Place in greased bowl, turning to grease top. Cover and let rise in warm place until doubled in size. Punch dough down and turn out onto lightly floured board and divide in half. Roll each piece of dough into a 24" rope. Twist ropes together loosely and form into a ring on a greased baking sheet. Brush with melted butter. Place colored eggs into spaces in the twist. Let rise in warm place until doubled, about 1 hour. Brush with melted butter.

Bake at 350°F about 30 – 35 minutes until done. Cool on wire rack.

I grew up in Estonia in eastern Europe, and I remember my grandmother making this bread for her grandchildren. We would carefully color the eggs, and once the dough was ready, we would place the eggs into the dough. While this recipe calls for five eggs, we never had more than three, as eggs could be very difficult to get.

Helgi Lunt, Atria Harborhill resident

Flo's Rocky Road

Prep Time: 15 minutes | Cook Time: 10 minutes | Servings: 50

Ingredients:

12 oz. semi-sweet chocolate chips
2 tbsp. margarine
1 (14 oz.) can sweetened condensed milk
2 c. dry roasted peanuts
1 (10 oz.) pkg. mini marshmallows

Preparation:

In a saucepan, melt chips, margarine and condensed milk.

Remove from heat. In a large bowl combine nuts and marshmallows.

Fold in the melted chips. Spread into a waxed, paper-lined 9"x 13" Pyrex® dish. Chill for 2 hours.

Cut into small squares and serve.

My "rocky road treats" have been on the "road" with me for over 35 years. They are a favorite treat for the holidays. I've made them for family, friends and my co-workers at the bank where I worked for over 40 years.

Florence Rovetti, Atria Lynbrook resident

Frozen Lime Pie

Prep Time: 20 minutes, plus freezing time | Servings: 6 – 8

Ingredients:

5 ½ oz. pkg. chocolate-covered graham crackers (about 12 crackers)

3 tbsp. butter or margarine, softened

2 eggs, separated

14 oz. sweetened condensed milk

1 tbsp. finely grated lime peel

⅔ c. lime juice (about 4 limes)

¼ c. sugar

Preparation:

Roll chocolate graham crackers between 2 pieces of waxed paper to make 1 ½ cups of crumbs. Combine crumbs with melted butter or margarine. Mix thoroughly. Press mixture evenly on bottom and sides of 9" pie plate.

Beat egg yolks until thick, combine with condensed milk, stir in lime juice and a little lime peel. Mix well.

In a separate bowl, beat egg whites until stiff, but not dry. Gradually add sugar and beat until very stiff. Fold into lime-milk mixture.

Turn into prepared pie plate. Place in freezer until firm, about 6 hours.

If desired, garnish with a frill of whipped cream and grated semi-sweet chocolate around the edge of the pie.

I found this recipe in the *Parade* food editor section of our newspaper in 1957 and decided to try it. It became a family favorite. A frozen pie makes a nice and cool summer dessert. I still have the original clipping!

Eunice Williams, Atria Merrimack Place resident

G.G.'s Rugelach

Prep Time: 45 minutes | Cook Time: 10 – 15 minutes | Servings: 50

Ingredients:

½ lb. cream cheese, softened
½ lb. butter or margarine, softened
2 c. flour
3 tbsp. sugar
¼ c. mix of sugar, cinnamon, crushed walnuts
½ c. raisins

Preparation:

Blend together cream cheese, butter, flour and sugar. Refrigerate until firm. Roll a handful of dough at a time on a floured board to approximately ¼" thickness.

With a knife, cut dough into tiny triangles about 3" long and 1 ½" wide at its base. Sprinkle triangles with sugar, cinnamon and ground walnuts to your liking. Put 1 raisin into each triangle and roll it up, starting at the base.

Bake at 350°F on an ungreased cookie sheet for 10 – 15 minutes or until lightly brown.

When I first met my husband over 20 years ago, he used to have these very interesting little empty tin canisters in the kitchen of his New York City apartment. As we continued to date and I met his parents, they too had these little empty tin containers on their kitchen counter. One day I expressed interest about these empty tins and I was told that Grandma Lille (G.G.) would bring them filled with her famous tiny rugelach. You needed to return your tins so that she would fill them again. Once married, I helped empty the tins every time we were lucky enough to have G.G. come visit. No one could ever make the rugelach as small as she could. (That meant that you could eat more since they were so small!)

Patricia Finkelberg, Atria on Roslyn Harbor Community Sales Director, pictured here with her husband, Howard

Gram's Christmas Cookies

Prep Time: 30 minutes | Cook Time: 10 – 15 minutes | Servings: 24

Ingredients:

Cookies:

3 c. brown sugar

½ lb. butter

1 c. Crisco® shortening

4 tbsp. vanilla extract

2 eggs

1 c. buttermilk (can substitute 1 heaping tsp. baking soda in regular milk)

3 c. flour

2 heaping tsp. baking powder

8 c. flour

Frosting:

¼ lb. butter

½ c. white Karo® syrup

3 tbsp. cream or milk (it might take more)

2 tsp. vanilla extract

2 lbs. powdered sugar, as needed to spread

food coloring (optional)

Preparation:

Cookies: Cream together the brown sugar, butter, shortening and vanilla. Add in the eggs and buttermilk and stir. Fold in flour and baking powder. Continue to add flour until soft dough forms, about 8 cups. Roll out dough on hard surface, using flour. Use any type of cookie cutter to cut out dough. Place on a cookie sheet and bake at 325°F for 10 – 15 minutes or until lightly brown. When done, remove from oven, and let cool before frosting.

Frosting: Mix butter, syrup, cream/milk, vanilla and powdered sugar until it reaches a creamy consistency. Stir in a few drops of food coloring if desired.

Memories of time spent at my grandmother's house are easily the most vivid of any in my childhood. Among our favorite times at Gram's were those days we spent baking her special cut-out cookies. I can still see all of us eagerly waiting as Mom or Gram took the cookies out of the oven; we were hoping that one of them would break, which meant we could eat it right away rather than wait for the frosting.

Probably most unique, though, is the memory of Gram and her broom… you see, these cookies were rolled in flour, and inevitably that flour would end up all over us. So, Gram would herd us onto the front porch and "sweep" us off with her broom. Boy, did we get a kick out of that!

The oldest cousin in our group always makes these cookies at Christmas and distributes them to all of us as we gather for our traditional Christmas Eve celebration. Family is important to us and there's nothing that defines and symbolizes the love in our family quite like Gram's Christmas cookies!

Julie Harding, Atria Senior Living Executive Vice President & Chief Operating Officer

Granddaddy's Brown Bread

Prep Time: 10 minutes | Cook Time: 30 minutes | Servings: 8

Ingredients:

- 2 c. stone-ground whole wheat flour (may use regular whole wheat)
- 1 tsp. baking soda
- 1 tsp. salt
- pinch of baking powder (optional)
- 3 tbsp. Crisco® shortening
- 1 ¼ c. buttermilk (add ¼ c. more, if needed)

Preparation:

Sift together dry ingredients. Blend in shortening. Add buttermilk and mix until blended. Add ¼ cup more buttermilk if necessary to ensure mix is moist but not runny.

Spread into a greased 10 ½" cast iron skillet, or Pyrex® dish if you don't have cast iron skillet.

Bake at 375°F for 30 minutes or until golden brown. Cut into 8 pie shapes and serve warm with butter.

Granddaddy Patton was born in 1877 in Watertown, Tennessee, and became a Presbyterian minister. My father, the youngest of five, was born in 1914. Granddaddy would drive out to our farm in South Carolina to help my mother, Kennon, with my sisters and me, and assist with meals. He enjoyed making brown bread in an iron skillet. Occasionally, he would take us to purchase the whole wheat flour directly from the mill. "Fresh stone-ground," he claimed, was the secret! He lived to be 106 ½. My children and grandchildren love the taste and you will, too!

Story submitted by Blair Patton Green, pictured here with her mother, Atria Lincoln Place resident Kennon Henderson Patton, and Blair's granddaughter, Aliza

Grandma Pep's Sour Cream Chocolate Chip Coffee Cake

Prep Time: 30 minutes | Cook Time: 1 hour | Servings: 8

Ingredients:

Cake:

1 c. butter

1 c. sour cream

1 c. sugar

1 ½ c. flour

1 ½ tsp. baking powder

1 tsp. baking soda

1 egg

Topping:

¼ c. brown sugar

1 (8 oz.) pkg. chocolate chips

Preparation:

Mix all cake ingredients. Mix topping ingredients separately. Make layers by pouring half of the cake batter into well-greased cake pan. Sprinkle half of topping mixture on batter.

Pour in remainder of the cake batter and top with the remainder of the topping mixture.

Bake at 350°F for 1 hour.

Note that using extra chips will cause cake to fall.

My Grandma Pepperman, or Grandma "Pep" as I called her, was a strong supporter of the City of Hope. The charity helped her sister-in-law who had tuberculosis, and she was cured with their help. Whenever she attended an event where a food contribution was requested, Grandma Pep brought her wonderful sour cream chocolate chip coffee cake. Many attendees would ask her for the recipe and her response was, "Give me a dollar for the City of Hope and I will be happy to share it." She made lots of money for her favorite charity this way.

Story submitted by Hedy Kirsh, pictured here with her mother, Atria Woodbridge resident Edna Davis

Hamantaschen

Prep Time: 3 – 4 hours | Cook Time: 20 minutes | Makes: 60

Ingredients:

Dough:
5 c. flour
1 c. sugar
2 tsp. baking powder
1 pinch of salt
1 lb. butter
5 tbsp. sour cream
2 tsp. lemon juice
2 tsp. vanilla extract
4 egg yolks
Filling:
1 jar apricot filling
1 jar prune filling
1 jar mohn (poppy seed) filling

Preparation:

Sift dry ingredients together (flour, sugar, baking powder and salt). In mixer, mix butter, sour cream, lemon juice, vanilla extract and well-beaten egg yolks. Pour in dry-ingredient mixture and mix to create dough. Divide dough into balls. Wrap in wax paper and put in refrigerator for a few hours (or overnight).

Roll out dough to ¼ " thickness. Using a round cutter, glass or scalloped cutter, cut circles in dough and fill with any of the fillings (about ½ to 1 teaspoonful) in the center of each circle. Fold up sides to make a three-sided cookie and pinch sides tightly together.

Place unbaked cookies in the freezer for half an hour.

Remove chilled cookies and bake in oven at 375°F for 20 minutes or until golden brown.

It was getting close to Purim, and the sisterhood of my synagogue called a meeting to teach all the young wives how to make hamantaschen. We were instructed by a very stern, older German woman, who lined us all up at the table and told us, in no uncertain terms, how to make the hamantaschen, per this recipe. I think we were all a little bit intimidated by her mannerisms. However, we all learned to make these delicious cookies, which have become a family favorite at all times of the year, not just Purim!

Betty Wolgel, Atria Cutter Mill resident

Hot Milk Cake

Prep Time: 30 minutes | Cook Time: 25 – 35 minutes | Servings: 16

Ingredients:

1 c. milk
1 stick butter
4 eggs
2 c. sugar
pinch of salt
2 c. of flour
2 tsp. vanilla
2 tsp. baking powder

Preparation:

Preheat oven to 400°F. Put milk and butter in a saucepan on low heat. Cook until butter melts. Do not boil.

In a large bowl, beat eggs. Add sugar gradually and then add salt. Add in the flour, being careful not to make the batter too thick. Add the milk and melted butter mixture gradually. Finish adding flour. Add vanilla and baking powder, then beat mixture well. Bubbles should appear.

Grease and flour pans. Pour into cake pans and put in oven 25 minutes for a layer cake or 35 minutes for a sheet cake.

Bake at 400°F or until done.

Allow cake to cool completely before adding your icing of choice.

This is an old German recipe from my great-grandmother. I learned how to bake it when I was eight years old. I was so proud of myself! On birthdays and special occasions, I would help my mom, Gwendolyn, make it. We iced it with vanilla, chocolate or orange icing. My mom loves it when I bring in her hot milk cake!

Story submitted my Cheryl Kirk, pictured here with her mother, Atria Salisbury resident Gwendolyn Wray

Hot Water Cornbread

Prep Time: 10 minutes | Cook Time: 15 minutes | Servings: 12

Ingredients:

1 c. water
pinch of salt
1 c. yellow cornmeal
1 tsp. bacon grease, plus 1 c. for frying

Preparation:

In a small sauce pan, boil 1 cup of water. Add a pinch of salt, 1 cup cornmeal and 1 teaspoon of bacon grease into the boiling water. Stir until the mixture becomes firm and the cornmeal absorbs all the water.

Remove pan from heat and set on a heat-safe surface near the sink. When mixture has cooled enough to handle, run your hands under cold water. Scoop 1 tablespoon of mixture and roll together using the palms of your hands. Flatten it slightly to make a patty. With your thumb, make a small indentation in the top of the patty. This will keep the patty from shrinking much while it cooks.

To fry the patties, heat 1 cup of bacon grease in a cast iron skillet. Carefully place 1 or 2 patties at a time into hot grease. Cook until they are a crispy golden brown on both sides and cooked all the way through.

This was my husband's grandmother's recipe. When we were first married, my husband asked me to learn how to cook his grandmother's famous cornbread. When I asked his Mamaw for the recipe, she said, "I don't measure when I make this recipe." As a young bride, I pleaded for her to write it down so I could cook it for my new husband. Mamaw and I stood in the kitchen together until it was written down. We loved serving these with sweet potatoes, mustard greens and fried pork chops. From our family to yours, I hope you enjoy this as much as we have for many years!

Pat Henderson, Atria Collier Park resident

Hungarian Pogácsa
Butter Cookies

Prep Time: 10 minutes | Cook Time: 15 – 20 minutes | Servings: 24

Ingredients:

5 c. flour
1 lb. butter
1 c. sugar
2 eggs, whole
2 egg yolks
1 c. sour cream
1 tsp. baking powder
½ tsp. salt

Preparation:

Blend flour and butter together. Add sugar, 2 whole eggs and 2 egg yolks and mix well. Add sour cream, baking powder and salt.

Roll dough on floured board about ¼ " thick. Using a round cookie cutter or a juice glass, cut the cookies; make crisscross marks on top of cookies with a fork.

Bake at 350°F for about 15 – 20 minutes until golden brown.

My mom made these cookies and she could compete with any of today's gourmet cooks. She had a pastry shop in Corona, Queens, New York and would stay up all night baking. She drove to deliver her baked goods the next day all by herself. Her baking was passed on to me, and it has been subsequently passed down to my daughters and granddaughters.

Jeannette Weledniger, Atria on Roslyn Harbor resident pictured here with her granddaughters, Lara and Allie Stahl

Jeff Davis Pie

Prep Time: 5 minutes | Cook Time: 20 – 30 minutes | Servings: 6 – 8

Ingredients:

2 c. sugar
1 c. milk
½ c. butter
4 egg yolks
½ tsp. vanilla
1 pastry crust

Preparation:

Mix sugar, milk, butter, egg yolks and vanilla. Pour batter into an open pastry crust.

Bake at 350°F until set.

Check for doneness after 20 minutes, as this usually takes around 20 – 30 minutes until set.

This recipe was given to me by my grandmother, who was born in 1856 in Alabama. This recipe dates back to the Civil War, hence the name of the President of the Confederate States of America, Jefferson Davis. Modern cooks will recognize this as a sweet dessert quiche. During and after the Civil War, this would have been what a farm housewife had in her cupboard when she could afford the sugar and vanilla.

Vera Burns Faubion, Atria Merrimack Place resident

Joe Frogger Cookies

Prep Time: 20 minutes | Cook Time: 10 – 12 minutes | Servings: 24

Ingredients:

7 c. flour
1 tbsp. salt
1 tbsp. fresh ginger
1 tsp. ground cloves
1 tsp. fresh nutmeg
1 tsp. allspice
¾ c. hot water
¼ c. rum
2 tsp. baking soda
2 c. very dark molasses
1 c. shortening
2 c. sugar

Preparation:

Sift together: flour, salt, ginger, clove, nutmeg and allspice. Combine hot water with rum. Combine baking soda with dark molasses. Cream shortening and sugar. Add sifted dry ingredients, the water-rum mixture and the molasses mixture to the creamed mixture, one half of each at a time.

Chill the dough, then roll out ¼" thick and cut with a 4" cutter.

Bake at 375°F for 10 – 12 minutes.

I'm from Marblehead, Massachusetts, where my family has lived for 13 generations. This recipe was passed down throughout the family. It is a joy to make and these cookies last longer than most others. The cookies are named for Joseph (Joe) Brown, locally recognized as a veteran of the revolution, as well as one of the first black business owners in the United States. Joe, a former slave, opened a tavern right by a pond, and his house has been preserved there. He ran the tavern with the help of his wife, Lucretia, who made the first "Joe Frogger" cookies. Marblehead's early fishermen used to take the cookies on long voyages as a standard part of their ship's provisions. The ingredients of rum and seawater acted as preservatives. While today the cookies are mostly round, in the beginning they were described as lily pad shaped.

Deb Caulkins, Atria Draper Place resident

Kugel

Prep Time: 20 minutes | Cook Time: 50 minutes | Servings: 8

Ingredients:

1 lb. egg noodles
1 ½ tsp. cinnamon
3 eggs
¼ c. sugar or Sweet'N Low®
1 c. raisins
½ c. pineapple, chunked
8 oz. cottage cheese
8 oz. sour cream
¼ c. bread crumbs

Preparation:

Cook noodles according to package directions and drain.

Mix all ingredients except bread crumbs in a large bowl.

Grease casserole dish and dust lightly with bread crumbs.

Place mixture in casserole dish.

Bake at 400°F degrees for 10 minutes. Reduce temperature to 375°F and bake an additional 40 minutes.

Cool for 10 minutes and serve.

My favorite dish is kugel. It is a traditional Hanukkah dish. My dad would make it for us every Hanukkah season. I loved it so much that he taught me how to make it at age 15. The kugel turned out so well that it became my job to prepare it every year.

Phyllis Waterman, Atria Marina Place resident

Lemon Cake

Prep Time: 15 minutes | Cook Time: 37 minutes | Servings: 12 – 15

Ingredients:

Cake:

1 lemon cake mix

1 small box lemon JELL-O®

3 large eggs

¾ c. cooking oil

Glaze:

½ c. lemon juice

1 lb. box powdered sugar

Preparation:

Blend cake mix, JELL-O, eggs and oil. Grease and flour a 9"x 13" cake pan. Bake at 350°F for 30 minutes until done.

While cake is baking, mix lemon juice and powdered sugar to make a glaze.

After 30 minutes, remove cake and pierce top with a fork in several places. Pour glaze over the cake, allowing it to soak in.

Return cake to oven for 7 more minutes.

A courtship of four weeks before a marriage proposal turned into 63 years of marriage. My husband, Paul, was in the Army Air Corps as a gunner, and after the war he became a fire captain. I was a schoolteacher and together we ran a very active household with six children. As the old cliché would say, "Firemen make great cooks." Paul was no exception. While off from the station, he enjoyed preparing for big events such as Thanksgiving dinner. He was also a fine dessert maker, with numerous recipes to choose from his proven track record! This is just one of them.

Betty Critchfield, Atria Del Sol resident

Lemon Pie

Prep Time: 20 minutes | Cook Time: 35 – 40 minutes | Servings: 8 – 10

Ingredients:

1 graham cracker pie crust
vanilla wafers, enough to line around edge of pie pan
3 eggs
14 oz. can sweetened condensed milk
¼ c. lemon juice, fresh squeezed and strained
3 tsp. sugar
4 oz. cream cheese (optional)

Preparation:

Line wafers around edge of pie crust, standing on their ends. Separate egg whites in a different bowl. Mix egg yolks, condensed milk and lemon juice in bowl. (For a thicker pie, mix in 4 ounces of cream cheese.) Pour into pie crust.

Bake 30 to 35 minutes or until set. Remove from oven. Let cool for 1 hour, then refrigerate for at least 3 hours.

Beat egg whites, adding sugar gradually for desired taste, until peaks form. Spread over pie and place in 400°F oven for 5 minutes until peaks are slightly browned.

Cool and refrigerate for several hours before serving.

Mother got this recipe from a lady that cooked for her family when she first got married in 1939! The cook got the recipe from her grandmother, so it was very old to begin with. Mother made this for her children and I made it for my children.

Story submitted by Meredith Austin, pictured here with her mother, Atria Westchase resident Alice Austin

Luvenia's Peach Cobbler

Prep Time: 15 minutes | Cook Time: 1 hour | Servings: 12

Ingredients:

2 (29 oz.) cans peaches

½ c. sugar

pinch of nutmeg

pinch of salt

⅓ c. butter

1 tsp. vanilla

3 ready-made pie crusts
(big enough to layer in a 9" x 13" pan)

Preparation:

Preheat oven to 350°F.

Line a 9" x 13" casserole dish with first pie crust dough. Mix peaches, sugar, nutmeg, salt, butter and vanilla in a large bowl (include liquid from canned peaches). Pour half of the peach mixture onto the bottom layer crust.

Cut 1 pie crust into strips and place the strips on top of mixture. Pour the rest of the peach cobbler on top of the strips. Top off cobbler with your third pie crust.

Spot crust with butter and sprinkle with sugar. Pinch the top and bottom crust edges together to seal.

Cook approximately 1 hour or until crust is brown. Let cool prior to serving. It's great with vanilla ice cream.

My mom's claim to fame in her hometown of St. Louis, Missouri was her peach cobbler. She must have made it no less than 100 times for each and every special event. This was her calling card. Of course, she started making the cobbler for special Sunday meals with the immediate family. As relatives and invited guests tasted this delicacy, the word got out, which meant that she had to make a large pan of peach cobbler whenever she appeared as a guest to other events. I believe that the invitations basically included Mom and the cobbler, as one could not arrive without the other.

Story submitted by Christine Sullivan, pictured here with her mother, Atria Bayside Landing resident Luvenia Fitzpatrick

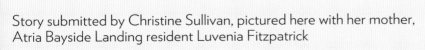

Macaroons

Prep Time: 15 minutes | Cook Time: 12 minutes | Servings: 12

Ingredients:

2 egg whites
pinch of salt
½ c. white sugar
2 c. sweetened flaked coconut

Preparation:

Preheat oven to 375°F.

Lightly grease a baking sheet.

Beat together the egg whites with the salt in a small bowl until it forms soft peaks. Add the sugar 1 tablespoon at a time while continuing to beat at high speed until stiff peaks form. Continue to beat until glossy. Fold the coconut into the egg mixture.

Drop mixture by the teaspoonful onto the prepared sheet, spacing about 2" apart.

Bake in preheated oven for about 12 minutes.

I grew up in Karpathos, Greece, an island in the Aegean Sea. Easter was the biggest holiday of the year for my family. My mother would make a large quantity of macaroons for our family and neighbors. Our family would enjoy eating the macaroons while we dyed hard-boiled eggs each year.

Maria Scoulos, Atria Woodbridge Place resident

Mom's Snowballs

Prep Time: 20 minutes | Cook Time: 10 – 15 minutes | Servings: 24

Ingredients:

1 c. butter
½ c. powdered sugar
1 tsp. vanilla
2 ¼ c. flour, sifted
¼ tsp. salt
¾ c. walnuts, ground

Preparation:

Cream butter in large bowl until light. Add powdered sugar, creaming well until mixture is light and fluffy. Stir in vanilla. Sift flour and salt together. Blend into creamed mixture.

Stir in walnuts.

Shape into balls the size of walnuts and place on ungreased cookie sheet.

Bake at 350°F for 10 – 15 minutes. Remove from cookie sheet and roll the balls in additional powdered sugar.

Cool on cookie rack. Once cooled, roll again in powdered sugar.

Double the recipe for a large crowd!

Christmas is not Christmas without my mom's snowball cookies. I love them! She prepared them for our family every Christmas, even when ingredients were hard to get in the many countries we lived in: Venezuela, Argentina, Indonesia, Mexico, Australia and Japan. My father was an executive with Goodyear Tire & Rubber Company, so we moved often. The snowballs made any place feel like home. This recipe was handed down from my mother's mother.

Story submitted by Mark Schlup, son of Atria Johnson Ferry resident Carolyn Schlup, pictured here

Oatmeal Bombers

Prep Time: 10 minutes | Cook Time: 10 – 12 minutes | Servings: 48

Ingredients:

⅓ c. margarine or butter, softened
½ c. Splenda®
2 eggs
1 c. unsweetened applesauce
1 tsp. vanilla
1 c. whole wheat flour
1 tsp. baking powder
½ tsp. baking soda
1 tsp. cinnamon
½ tsp. salt
1 c. quick or old-fashioned oatmeal, uncooked
½ c. raisins (optional)

Preparation:

Preheat oven to 350°F.

Beat together margarine and Splenda until creamy. Add eggs and vanilla, beat well. Add flour, baking soda and cinnamon and mix well.

Stir in oats and raisins.

Drop by rounded tablespoons onto an ungreased cookie sheet.

Bake 10 – 12 minutes until golden brown.

I've never been one to back down from a challenge. In 1942 I joined the United States Army Air Corps, becoming a bomber pilot. I flew a total of 65 missions for the Allied Forces: 33 on the B-25s and 32 on the B-24s. So, when I was diagnosed with diabetes, I was ready to face the challenge head on, just as I faced my missions: with courage and determination. I try to take care of myself by exercising daily and eating right. This sugar-free recipe is one of my favorites. Enjoy!

Dorman Dane, Atria Summit Ridge resident

Passover Rolls

Prep Time: 50 minutes | Cook Time: 1 hour | Servings: 8

Ingredients:

½ c. vegetable oil or shortening
1 c. water
2 c. matzoh meal
4 eggs

Preparation:

In a pan, bring water to boil and add oil. Add matzoh meal.

Beat rapidly over low heat until mixture leaves sides of pan and forms a ball.

Remove from heat. Beat in eggs one at a time. Beat hard until batter is thick and smooth.

Shape into 8 balls and place on well-greased baking sheet. With a butter knife, cut an "X" on the top of each.

Bake at 350°F for 1 hour.

Our family started making these Passover rolls as a nice change from matzoh. My sister-in-law, who taught me how to cook and bake, showed me how to make this recipe. She passed it down to me and I passed it down to my daughter-in-laws.

Shirley Daichman, Atria Tinton Falls resident

Pea-Picking Pineapple Cake

Prep Time: 5 minutes | Cook Time: 30 minutes | Servings: 8 – 10

Ingredients:

cooking spray
1 box yellow cake mix
1 (8 oz.) can mandarin oranges
½ c. vegetable oil
4 large eggs
2 tsp. vanilla
1 (16 oz.) tub Cool Whip®
1 large can crushed pineapple
1 box instant vanilla pudding

Preparation:

Spray three 9" cake pans with cooking spray.

Mix the following ingredients together in a large bowl with an electric mixer for 3 minutes: yellow cake mix, mandarin oranges, vegetable oil, 4 large eggs and 1 teaspoon vanilla.

Then pour the batter into three 9" greased cake pans.

Bake for 30 minutes at 350°F. Cool for approximately 30 minutes.

While cake is cooling, mix together Cool Whip, crushed pineapples, instant vanilla pudding and 1 teaspoon vanilla in a medium-sized bowl. Refrigerate for about 5 – 10 minutes.

When cake is cool, frost layers with Cool Whip mixture, assemble and refrigerate until ready to serve. Enjoy!

This recipe was given to me by my sister, Mary Joe. It is called pea-picking cake because it is so easy to make, that you could pick peas all day and go home and make it and have it ready for dinner that night. This is a favorite dessert of my granddaughters for their birthdays and other family gatherings.

Margaret Yancey, Atria Evergreen Woods resident

Pennsylvania Dutch Taffy

Prep Time: 5 – 7 minutes | Cook Time: 10 – 20 minutes | Servings: 1 ¼ pounds

Ingredients:

1 bottle Karo® syrup, prefer dark
2 c. sugar, granulated
½ stick butter or margarine
1 tsp. vanilla
pinch of cream of tartar or baking soda
*a candy thermometer is recommended for this recipe

Preparation:

Place all ingredients together in a large saucepan. Bring to a boil, stirring constantly, until mix reaches the soft-crack stage at 270°F, or forms pliable threads when a bit is dropped into cold water. Carefully pour mix onto a butter-greased cookie sheet.

Butter hands well to keep the hot candy from sticking to your fingers. As soon as possible, handle the taffy. Start pulling good-sized handfuls from the edges. Pull as hard and as quickly as possible; speed is important. Keep buttering hands as needed. Pull until the candy is honey-blonde in color, almost white.

Shape into a rope about as wide as your finger. Place rope on another butter-greased cookie sheet. Continue to pull off handfuls and create more ropes until you run out of mixture.

When taffy is all pulled, cut into 1" lengths with buttered kitchen scissors.

If the candy is too hard to cut due to overcooking or poor pullers, you will have to crack it into pieces. It's still delicious, but warn your guests not to chew when you serve it!

As a child, we didn't make taffy often, but it was a memorable event. You need a group of people to make taffy because once it's cooked, it has to be pulled. That's why it's called a "taffy pull" when people get together to make it.

After it was cooked, my mother would take a handful of gooey taffy and pull it until it had cooled off a little. Once it was cool enough for the rest of the of us to handle, she'd let us pull the taffy some more. The more you pull the taffy, the better it melts in your mouth when you eat it!

Story submitted by Jan Rohn, daughter of Atria Tinton Falls resident Joan Thiers, pictured here

Potato Chip Cookies

Prep Time: 15 minutes | Cook Time: 15 – 20 minutes | Servings: 48

Ingredients:

1 lb. butter, softened
1 c. sugar
3 ¼ c. flour
1 tsp. vanilla extract
1 ½ c. potato chips, coarsely crushed (non-fat ridges preferred)
confectioners' sugar

Preparation:

Cream butter and sugar. Slowly blend in flour and vanilla extract. Gently mix in chips. (If mix is too crumbly, you may add milk.)

Drop batter by well-rounded teaspoon onto cookie sheet. Lightly flatten with fork and make as thin as possible.

Bake at 325°F for 15 – 20 minutes.

At 15 minutes, check cookies; they should be lightly browned on the bottom. If not, continue baking an additional few minutes.

Remove from heat and let cool.

Sprinkle with confectioners' sugar.

My mom used to work the election polls in the city of Bethlehem. She volunteered for all kinds of elections: local, state and national. One time, a fellow poll worker brought in these cookies and they were a big hit! I usually make them at Christmas time. They do have somewhat of a following considering potato chips are part of the ingredients. It's hard to stop after eating one!

Story submitted by Lori Zabrecky, daughter of Atria Bethlehem resident Mary Zabrecky, pictured here

Pumpkin Bread

Prep Time: 15 minutes | Cook Time: 50 minutes | Servings: 3 loaves

Ingredients:

4 eggs

2 ⅔ c. sugar

1 stick margarine

⅔ c. water

1 (15 oz.) can pumpkin

3 ⅓ c. flour

½ tsp. baking powder

2 tsp. baking soda

1 tsp. cinnamon

1 tsp. ground clove

1 c. raisins (light or dark)

Preparation:

Preheat oven to 350°F. Cream eggs, sugar and margarine together. Add water and pumpkin. Mix. In separate bowl, combine flour, baking powder, baking soda, cinnamon and clove. Add dry ingredients a cup at a time to the wet ingredients, mixing each cup thoroughly. Add raisins and mix through. Apply cooking spray to three 7"x 3" pans. (Optionally, you can pour batter into soup cans half full, allowing room for bread to rise.) Pour in batter and bake for 50 minutes or until a toothpick can be inserted into the bread and cleanly removed.

Pumpkin bread is one of the first baked goods my mom taught me to cook. My mom and I both have a sweet tooth, so maybe that's why she started teaching with goodies. Mom taught me to always bake the loaves in coffee cans and I thought nothing of it. She's a New England girl, so using a can for baking was reminiscent of Boston brown bread that is baked in a can. When I first moved out on my own, coffee cans made loaves that were too large, so I switched to Progresso® soup cans. I can make five smaller loaves instead of three – more to share with friends. This item is our "go to" fall treat, from the moment the cool air hits, right through to Christmas. The year I moved to Florida, I was homesick and especially missed the seasons. When fall rolled around, I made pumpkin bread and shared the loaves at work. I explained that I baked them in the soup cans (which is obvious when you remove the loaves from the cans). My co-worker, a southern belle who'd lived all her life in Florida, asked me if my family was so poor that we had to bake food using cans. I had a good laugh and said it's an old New England thing! However you choose to bake your pumpkin bread, it will become a much-loved treat. From our kitchen to yours, enjoy!

Story submitted by Sandie Miller, pictured here with her mother, Atria Guilderland resident Barbara Miller, and her sister Robin Goodrich

Pumpkin Cake with Cream Cheese Icing

Prep Time: 30 minutes | Cook Time: 40 – 50 minutes | Servings: 16

Ingredients:

Cake:

3 eggs

2 c. sugar

2 c. canned pumpkin (not pie filling)

½ c. vegetable oil

½ c. applesauce (sugar-free)

2 tsp. cinnamon

2 tsp. baking soda

2 tsp. baking powder

½ tsp. salt

1 c. flour

1 tsp. vanilla extract

Icing:

1 stick butter

1 (8 oz.) pkg. Kraft Philadelphia® cream cheese

1 lb. confectioners' sugar

2 tsp. vanilla extract

2 – 3 c. pecans, chopped

Preparation:

Cake: Combine eggs, sugar, pumpkin, oil and applesauce. Mix in cinnamon, baking soda, baking powder, salt, flour and vanilla. Beat for 2 minutes.

Grease two 9" round pans and dust with flour.

Pour batter into pans.

Bake at 350°F for 30 – 35 minutes. Check center with toothpick periodically for doneness.

Icing: Bring butter to room temperature. Mix with cream cheese, confectioners' sugar and vanilla.

Pecan topping: Bake pecans in oven at 350°F for 10 – 12 minutes.

Allow cake to cool completely before applying icing and coating with pecans.

My wife, Sue, used to make these cakes at Christmastime and give them out as gifts – family members, neighbors, the auto mechanic, the postman – you get the drift. Every year, everyone eagerly awaited Sue Hodges' beloved pumpkin cake.

Roland Hodges,
Atria Summit Hills resident

Pumpkin Chiffon Pie

Prep Time: 1 hour | Cook Time: 4 minutes | Servings: 8

Ingredients:

1 pkg. Knox® gelatin
¼ c. cold water
1 ⅓ c. canned pumpkin
½ c. milk
1 ½ tsp. ginger
1 ½ tsp. nutmeg
1 ½ tsp. cinnamon
1 ½ tsp. salt
3 eggs, separated
1 c. sugar, divided
1 ready-made pie crust

Preparation:

Bake pie crust according to package directions.

Combine gelatin and cold water. Set aside.

Cook pumpkin, milk, spices, salt, egg yolks and ¾ cup sugar over medium heat, stirring constantly, for 3 – 4 minutes until the mixture thickens.

Gently stir-in gelatin/water mixture and place mixture in refrigerator to partially set.

Beat 3 egg whites until stiff, adding ¼ cup sugar toward the end. Fold gently into the pumpkin mixture. Pour into pre-baked pie crust and chill until served (a full 24 hours is recommended).

Note: Extra gelatin will make a firmer pie. When the recipe is tripled, we use 4 packages of gelatin.

The origin of this recipe is lost in time, but it has been served at almost every Thanksgiving and Christmas in my family for at least 60 years. One funny memory is the year that my brother-in-law put Reddi-wip® on his slice of pie, and the Reddi-wip went on with such force that it went through the filling, hit the crust and then sprayed all over his mother across the table. We were lucky that it was her son and not one of the grandchildren who did it because she was not amused. We still laugh about it to this day.

Betty Nichols, Atria Briarcliff Manor resident

Refrigerator Cookies

Prep Time: 15 minutes + overnight | Cook Time: 10 minutes | Servings: 3

Ingredients:

¾ c. lard (Crisco®)
2 c. light brown sugar
2 eggs, beaten
2 tsp. vanilla flavoring
3 ½ c. flour
2 tsp. baking powder
½ tsp. salt
1 c. pecans, chopped

Preparation:

Mix together Crisco, sugar and salt.

Add in beaten eggs and vanilla.

Combine flour and baking powder, then add to the mixture.

Fold in pecans.

Divide batter into 3 portions and shape into rolls on slightly floured wax paper.

Wrap tightly and place in refrigerator overnight.

Preheat oven to 350°F. With a sharp knife, slice rolls into very thin cookies and place on a slightly greased cookie sheet.

Bake for 10 minutes or until lightly browned.

At my home, my mom made sure the cookie jar was never empty! There were always rolls of dough in the refrigerator waiting to be sliced thin and baked. Any time she visited, Mom always filled the cookie jar soon after she arrived.

Ruby Byrum, Atria MerryWood resident

Rhubarb Muffins

Prep Time: 25 minutes | Cook Time: 15 minutes | Servings: 12 – 16

Ingredients:

- 1 ¼ c. brown sugar
- ½ c. vegetable oil
- 1 egg
- 2 tsp. vanilla extract
- 1 c. buttermilk
- 1 ½ c. rhubarb, diced
- ½ c. nuts, chopped
- 2 ½ c. flour
- 1 tsp. baking soda
- 1 tsp. baking powder
- ½ tsp. salt

Preparation:

In large bowl, mix sugar, oil, egg, vanilla and buttermilk.

Add diced rhubarb and chopped nuts, then mix again.

Add in flour, baking soda and baking powder. Mix well.

Pour batter into muffin cups, filling each cup ¾ of the way to allow room for rising.

Bake muffins at 350°F for 15 minutes.

This was my grandmother's recipe. She grew her own rhubarb and every season she would make her rhubarb muffins. My grandmother even won a few blue ribbons at the county fair with this recipe. It was always a favorite of mine as a little girl.

Anabelle Doerr, Atria Golden Creek resident

Rum Cream Pie

Prep Time: 25 minutes | Servings: 2 pies

Ingredients:

6 egg yolks
1 c. sugar
1 envelope Knox® gelatin
½ c. water
1 pt. whipping cream
⅓ c. white rum
9" graham cracker crust
chocolate shavings or graham cracker crumbs (optional topping)

Preparation:

Mix egg yolks with sugar and beat for 3 minutes with electric beater until very creamy.

Dissolve Knox® gelatin slowly with ½ cup of water and bring to a boil.

Combine with egg mixture and let cool about 5 minutes.

Fold stiffly peaked whipped cream into egg mixture. Stir in white rum.

Pour into 9" graham cracker crust.

Chill at least 2 hours.

Before serving, grate chocolate on top or sprinkle with graham cracker crumbs.

This recipe is an all-time favorite in our family. It was something my mother would make for holidays or special occasions. Sometimes guests would come to the house and before they even had dinner they would ask, "Did you make rum cream pie?" My mother would smile and say, "Yes." You could be sure that everyone saved room when they knew what was for dessert. She would often make an extra pie or two and send one off with a relative who she knew was particularly fond of this tasty treat.

As time passed, it became a tradition to have rum cream pie for most special occasions. After my mother passed away, we continued to make this recipe for family gatherings. It is still something we all look forward to very much. The sweet memories of a very special mother linger in each bite.

Kathy Hazelton, Atria Woodbriar Engage Life Director

Sea Foam Candy

Prep Time: 15 minutes | Servings: 24

Ingredients:

- 2 egg whites
- 1 box light brown sugar
- 1 c. white sugar
- ¾ c. water
- 1 tsp. vinegar
- 1 tsp. vanilla extract

Preparation:

Beat egg whites in a mixing bowl and set aside.

Combine sugars, water and vinegar and stir over low heat until sugar dissolves.

Cook without stirring to 250°F or until small amount dropped in cold water form a very firm, but not brittle, ball.

Slowly pour over stiffly beaten egg whites, beating constantly with rotary beater until creamy.

Add vanilla.

Beat until mixture holds its shape.

Add nuts if desired.

Drop by teaspoon fulls onto wax paper and let harden.

Store in refrigerator.

This recipe is very old and I remember making it as a child. It was my father's favorite candy. Don't make it on a rainy day or it will flop!

Lois Neubrand, Atria Windsor Woods resident

Shoo-Fly Pie

Prep Time: 20 minutes | Cook Time: 30 – 40 minutes | Servings: 8

Ingredients:

1 ready-made 9″ pie shell
Crumb Mixture:
1 ½ c. flour
¾ c. sugar
¼ c. shortening
Molasses Mixture:
½ c. water
½ c. dark molasses
½ tsp. baking soda

Preparation:

Bring water to boil and mix in molasses. Then add baking soda and mix well.

Mix together crumb ingredients. In a separate bowl, mix together molasses ingredients. Combine ¾ of the crumb mixture with the molasses mixture and stir carefully. It should resemble the consistency of a cake batter. Pour molasses mixture into pie shell. Sprinkle remaining crumb mixture on top.

Bake at 350°F for 30 – 40 minutes. Periodically test with a toothpick: when it comes out clean, your pie is done. This will be a dry-bottom shoo-fly pie.

Shoo-fly pie can be a delicious dessert or a favorite addition to breakfast in our family. It makes a wonderful compliment to any breakfast along with a cup of hot coffee. Shoo-fly pie is not truly a pie, but more like a "sweet." Our family likes these pies at breakfast, lunch, dinner or as a snack. My dad's favorite evening snack was a slice of this delicious treat.

Believe it or not, I have known a member of my family to bake six or more shoo-flies on Saturday morning, and by Monday morning they would all have disappeared. After my mother died, Dad adjusted the recipe to make shoo-fly cupcakes. He later baked shoo-fly pies in 6″ pie pans. Oh, for a slice of warm shoo-fly pie and a cup of coffee right now!

Fred Livingood, Atria Salisbury resident

Steamed Chocolate Pudding

Prep Time: 30 – 45 minutes | Cook Time: 1 hour | Servings: 6 – 8

Ingredients:

Pudding:

1 c. flour

1 tsp. baking powder

⅛ tsp. salt

⅛ tsp. baking soda

½ c. sugar

1 tbsp. butter

1 egg, beaten

2 squares Baker's® unsweetened chocolate, melted

1 tsp. vanilla extract

½ c. milk

Sauce:

2 c. powdered sugar

1 egg, beaten

2 tsp. vanilla extract

5 tbsp. butter

1 c. cream, whipped

Preparation:

Pudding: Mix together flour, baking powder, salt and baking soda.

In a separate bowl, blend sugar, butter and beaten egg.

Add melted chocolate and vanilla. Add milk and flour mixture, alternating between the two a little bit at a time.

Pour batter into buttered pudding pan. Steam at least 1 hour. Serve on plate.

Sauce: Mix sugar, egg, melted butter and vanilla. Fold in whipped cream and mix gently until fluffy.

Serve pudding cake sliced, with a large ladle of sauce on each piece. Pass sauce to guests as they will want to add more!

This recipe has been in our family for quite some time, and my mother would make it for special occasions.

The sauce was so good, my daughter, Lee, once teased her sister, Pam, by purposely passing the sauce to everyone except Pam. Lee took great joy in seeing her sister get increasingly nervous that by the time the delicious sauce reached her, it might be all gone. After that, we always made extra.

Jean Watson, Atria Valley Manor resident

Strawberries a la Colony

Prep Time: 1 hour | Servings: 8 – 10

Ingredients:

1 pt. vanilla ice cream, softened
1 c. heavy cream, whipped
½ tsp. almond extract
1 qt. strawberries, quartered
½ c. sugar
⅓ c. Cointreau®

Preparation:

Mix ice cream, heavy cream and almond extract.

If preparing ahead of time, freeze at this point, then thaw in refrigerator before serving.

Gently toss cleaned strawberries, sugar and Cointreau together.

Refrigerate 1 hour, stirring occasionally.

Fold berries into cream mixture.

While in the Army in 1960, my husband, along with our family, served a three-year tour of duty, living in Paris. Our favorite dessert was this recipe, and it was usually served at dinner parties.

When we returned to the States, we visited family in Kansas City, Missouri. For dinner one evening, my husband's mother was making strawberry shortcake. When she finished, my daughter, Susanne, said, "My mom doesn't fix strawberries like that." Grandma was interested and asked, "How does she fix them?" Susanne replied, "She puts whiskey on the strawberries."

This story is told nearly every time we have had this dessert since that memorable comment.

Roberta Haynes, Atria Springdale resident

Swedish Nut Rolls

Prep Time: 30 minutes, then let dough stand overnight
Cook Time: 20 – 30 minutes | Servings: 48 rolls

Ingredients:

1 tsp. sugar

1 large yeast cake

1 c. milk, lukewarm

2 eggs, well beaten

1 c. oleo or margarine

½ c. sugar

4 c. flour

1 tsp. salt

Nut Filling:

1 lb. walnuts, ground

1 ½ c. brown sugar

1 c. milk

Preparation:

Grind the walnuts. In a medium-sized pot, add brown sugar, milk and nuts. Cook until mixture has thickened. Remove from stove and cool completely.

Mix together 1 teaspoon sugar, yeast cake, milk and eggs. In a separate bowl, mix together oleo, ½ cup sugar, flour and salt as you would pie dough. Mix the first bowl with the second and refrigerate overnight.

Divide dough into 4 sections with each section being a 12" circle. Spread with nut filling and let rise. Cut each circle into 12 slices, as you would a pie. Then roll each section, starting with the widest end to create a crescent roll.

Bake 350°F for 20 – 30 minutes, until golden brown.

My mother was a great baker and she would make these quite often. They were her favorite! The oven had a window in the front and we used to gather around and watch the rolls bake. I made them for my kids and now they make them for their children. It is a winner with our family!

Thelma Lingenfelter, Atria Greece resident

Wash Day Peach Cobbler

Prep Time: 15 minutes | Cook Time: 45 minutes | Servings: 6

Ingredients:

1 stick oleo
1 c. sugar
1 c. flour
1 c. milk
2 tsp. baking powder
15 ½ oz. can sliced peaches

Preparation:

Melt oleo in an 8" square pan.

Mix sugar, flour, milk and baking powder in a separate bowl.

Pour mixture into melted oleo.

Drop the peaches and juice in dollops over the mixed ingredients.

Bake at 350°F for 45 minutes.

When I was a child, Monday was wash day and the laundry was done in our back yard. The laundry equipment consisted of a large black pot over a bed of fire to heat the water, a broomstick to stir the dirty clothes, lye soap and two galvanized wash tubs filled with water for the clothes to be rinsed in. It was a sun-up to sun-down chore, leaving no time to make a complicated dessert. This recipe is quick and easy. The fragrance of it baking lingers in my memory.

Betty Dean, Atria Sugar Land resident

Zucchini Bread

Prep Time: 20 minutes | Cook Time: 1 hour, 20 minutes | Servings: 24

Ingredients:

3 eggs
2 c. sugar, white
1 c. vegetable oil
2 c. zucchini, grated
½ c. sour cream
3 c. all-purpose flour
¼ tsp. baking powder
1 tsp. baking soda
1 tsp. cinnamon, ground

Preparation:

Preheat oven to 350°F. Grease two 9"x 5" loaf pans.

Beat together eggs, sugar and oil.

Blend in the grated zucchini and then the sour cream.

Mix in the flour, baking powder, baking soda and cinnamon.

Pour batter into prepared pans.

Bake for 1 hour, 20 minutes at 350°F.

Let cool.

My husband Fritz was full of fun. He had our three children help him cook and bake this bread. They peeled the zucchini and chopped it up for this recipe (he chopped it finer when they were not looking). When the bread was finished and cool, they got to butter it, and of course eat the still-warm bread dripping in butter. Our children are in their 60's now and still talk about "Dad's cooking lessons." Of course, I was the one who got to clean up…

Anne Brunetti, Atria Daly City resident

A special thank you

Atria Senior Living would like
to thank all of our sponsors
who helped to make
A Dash & a Dollop
possible. Your generosity is
greatly appreciated.

Gold Sponsors:

Silver Sponsors: